SERVICES FOR THE URBAN POOR

SERVICES FOR THE URBAN POOR

A Select Bibliography

Richard Franceys
and Andrew Cotton

Intermediate Technology Publications
in association with the
Water, Engineering and Development Centre
1993

IT Publications, 103/105 Southampton Row, London WC1B 4HH, UK.
WEDC, Loughborough University of Technology, Leicestershire, LE11 3TU, UK.

ISBN 1 85339 188 3

Printed by Audio Visual Services (Loughborough University of Technology) Ltd.

ACKNOWLEDGEMENT

The work carried out by Richard Franceys, Andrew Cotton and Lawrence Hedderley on the infrastructure study and preparation of the bibliography was funded by the Overseas Development Administration (Project No. 4404) whose support is gratefully acknowledged.

CONTENTS

INTRODUCTION

RECENT FIGURES for the 'Low-Income' and 'Middle-Income Countries' (WDR, 1992) suggest that there is an urban population in the region of 1815 million. Of these, best estimates indicate that at least 30 per cent, that is 550 million people, will be living in informal housing, that is housing not sanctioned or approved according to government standards.

Considering a fifteen-year design horizon, the urban population in 2007 will be 3700 million people at present long-term growth rates. Therefore housing and infrastructure could be required for an additional 2500 million people (roughly equivalent to 385 million houses) if we are to achieve housing for all within fifteen years.

If conventional infrastructure standards are adopted, with household water supply, sewerage, solid waste collection, drainage and surfaced roads, the total annual cost per household (discounted lifecycle costs) is in the region of $133 for these services based on costs from a sample project in South-east Asia.

This figure does not necessarily represent the amount which a household has to pay in order to obtain these services but it does represent the amount which has to be paid by somebody, either through subsidies to a utility or other cross-subsidization through taxation of richer households in addition to user tariffs.

The affordability gap

However, the total annual income per household for the poorest 40 per cent of the population in the 'Low-Income Countries' is approximately $700. With affordability normally estimated in the region of 20 per cent for housing and services the total available annual expenditure is $140. It should be noted that this is a generous affordability percentage as studies show that the poorest can afford to spend least, even as a percentage.

Taking assumed minimum standards for a simple house suggests an annual cost per household of $100. Adding this figure to the amount required for conventional services indicates a cost of $233 per household which is substantially in excess of presumed affordability. The normal solution of cross-subsidization within a country is difficult where income-distribution figures indicate such a high percentage of low-income households.

Willingness to pay

It is therefore necessary to reconsider the objectives and means of providing infrastructure. The objectives may be considered to be an attempt, primarily through the built environment, to obtain health benefits, security and social requirement benefits and lastly convenience and status benefits.

Housing and infrastructure standards reflect differing costs, risks and benefits. However, there is confusion between objectives and means; whilst health benefits are often used to justify investments there is little evidence to suggest 'what benefit' accrues from 'what investment'. As time passes and professionals learn by failures there is a tendency for standards to be raised. This does not necessarily mean that previous 'lower' standards are 'wrong', they simply carry a higher risk in health and safety terms. Even existing 'conventional' standards, for all their high cost, are not risk free. Therefore the means of infrastructure provision should be more consistently related to the objectives.

In addition some mechanism has to be available to enable householders to demonstrate what they are willing to pay for. Too many sites and services schemes have imposed a level of convenience that people are not willing to pay for. This usually leads to a lack of maintenance and subsequent failure in some way of the infrastructure. Alternatively repayment terms have been set such that low-income householders are excluded from the development.

Putting services in their place

Consequently this bibliography details sources of information on infrastructure for low-income housing which can be considered as appropriate. Infrastructure needs to be seen as a service to support people and their housing rather than dominating in terms of costs. Technology choice is vital to achieve the correct balance of services to suit the particular needs of any location. Many of the techniques described in the publications listed here can be used to determine effective and efficient services for the poorest which are at the same time affordable and for which householders are willing to pay.

Referring to the South-east Asia project again, using on-plot sanitation, standposts, unpaved roads and storm drains, the cost of a simple level of services provision which retains environmental health benefits has a total annual cost per household of $43 compared with the $133. This is within a range of affordability and has the potential for upgrading as the household desires and is willing to pay. Further information on the research project leading to this bibliography can be found in *Services for Shelter* (Cotton and Franceys, 1991).

The bibliography

This bibliography is the result of a review of the literature on infrastructure design for urban low-income housing. The focus of the references which have been included is on the provision of site-level infrastructure appropriate for sites and services schemes, slum improvement programmes, and urban area upgrading programmes. The subjects covered are infrastructure planning, site preparation, drainage, roads and access, water supply, power supply, sanitation and solid waste management.

The bibliography will be of direct use to general, civil and public health engineers, urban planners, architects, and research workers who are involved in projects or programmes which have components of infrastructure provision.

The material found was predominantly concerned with conventional services provision on larger plot sizes; in addition the large amount of information on sanitation had a similar bias towards large plot sizes or towards rural development. There was a noticable lack of information directly related to the needs of low-income urban housing (reflecting the lack of previous research in this area). Where background information relating to conventional urban engineering or rural technology was thought to be relevant to the particular needs of low-income urban services, it has been included.

Conclusion

Careful attention to design of services can bring housing and infrastructure within the range of affordability of low-income households in the growing cities of the low-income countries. Reductions in cost can be achieved when compared with a conventional sites and services scheme of between 14 per cent and 68 per cent. These figures are significant when multiplied by the number of households which need to be established over the next fifteen years. It is hoped that the ideas and information referenced in this bibliography will enable planners and engineers to find out what has worked on other parts of the world, and to limit the common practise of over-designing so that there can be a better matching of the costs to the benefits while allowing the community the chance of upgrading at their own rate.

Richard Franceys and Andrew Cotton,
Water, Engineering and Development Centre,
Loughborough University of Technology, 1993

References

Cotton, A. P. and Franceys, R. W. A., *Services for Shelter*, Liverpool University Press, 1992.

WDR, 1992, *World Development Report 1992*, World Bank, Washington.

Section 1. INFRASTRUCTURE

1101

LOCATION OF UNDERGROUND SERVICES

BRUCE R.

PROCEEDINGS OF THE INSTITUTION OF MUNICIPAL AND
COUNTY ENGINEERS
VOL LXXIII 1947 p409-415
INSTITUTE OF MUNICIPAL ENGINEERS LONDON

The interaction between positioning of water supply, sewers,
electricity and gas services and the problems posed by tree roots in
the verges.

WATER SUPPLY/ELECTRICITY SUPPLY/SEWERS/
SERVICE LOCATION/UK

1102

DESIGN OF URBAN SPACE
GREATER LONDON COUNCIL MANUAL

CARTWRIGHT R.M. 1980 pp163

ARCHITECTURAL PRESS LONDON
HALSTED PRESS DIVISION JOHN WILEY NEW YORK

A design manual based on UK practice covering the problems of
urban space and including such aspects as water and drainage, road
construction, parking and junction layouts. Consideration is also
given to footpath design, lighting and street furniture.

DRAINAGE/ROADS/PARKING/FOOTPATHS/
STREET LIGHTING/ACCESS/UK

1103

SERVICES FOR SHELTER
PHYSICAL INFRASTRUCTURE FOR LOW-INCOME URBAN
HOUSING

COTTON A.P.
FRANCEYS R.W. A.   (under preparation) 1991

LIVERPOOL UNIVERSITY PRESS

A technical introduction to the physical infrastructure required on
low-income housing sites also detailing the interactions between
different sectors. Includes an approach to infrastructure provision
based on involving householders in the provision and upgrading
of technical services.

GROUND PREPARATION/DRAINAGE/ACCESS/ROADS/
WATER SUPPLY/SANITATION/SOLID WASTE/
POWER SUPPLY/UPGRADING/

COMMUNITY PARTICIPATION/INTERACTIONS

1104

TOWARDS GUIDELINES FOR SERVICES AND AMENITIES
IN DEVELOPING COMMUNITIES

CSIR   1988

DEPARTMENT OF DEVELOPMENT AID
PRETORIA Sections A-M

A loose-leaf publication applicable to all forms of development
from transition settlements and basic sites and services schemes to
conventional low-cost housing. The guidelines provide
information about a variety of relevant standards.

PLANNING/STORMWATER OPTIONS/ACCESS/TRANSPORTATION/
WATER SUPPLY/SANITATION/SOLID WASTE/ENERGY/
SOUTH AFRICA

1105

URBAN PLANNING AND DESIGN CRITERIA

de CHIARA J.
KOPPELMAN L. 1982 pp723

VAN NOSTRAND REINHOLD
NEW YORK

This reference book provides design guidelines on practical issues
in urban planning including urban design, housing, sub-division
and land development, and the design and location of public and
private utilities. Aspects of sewerage and solid waste disposal are
also covered with reference to US practice.

FIRE HYDRANTS/STREET LIGHTING/OPEN SPACES/
ROADS/PARKING/FOOTPATHS/FLOOD PREVENTION/
WATER SUPPLY/WATER STORAGE/POWER LINES/
SEWERS/SOLID WASTE/USA

1106

BUILDING REGULATIONS FOR HAPPY AND HEALTHY
LIVING

HYDERABAD DIRECTOR OF TOWN PLANNING 1972
pp112

DIRECTOR OF TOWN PLANNING
HYDERABAD
ANDHRA PRADESH
INDIA

This comic review of building regulations covers the growth in
cities against the background and history of the building and
planning regulations. Reference is made to road layouts and

widths, clearances and requirements for the siting of public services such as sewerage, electricity and water supply.

ROADS/SLOPING SITES/SANITATION/WATER SUPPLY/
BUILDING REGULATIONS/INDIA

1107

INDIAN PRACTICAL CIVIL ENGINEERS' HANDBOOK

KHANNA P N   12TH EDITION 1990

ENGINEERS' PUBLISHERS
NEW DELHI

An encyclopaedia of civil engineering knowledge, theory, practice and standards ideally suited to the needs of low-income countries and communities.

STRUCTURES/FOUNDATIONS/SOIL MECHANICS/
GROUND FILL/HYDRAULICS/WATER SUPPLY/DRAINAGE/
SEWERAGE/ROADS/POWER SUPPLY

1108

LOW-COST HOUSING

NATIONAL BUILDING RESEARCH INSTITUTE, REPUBLIC
OF SOUTH AFRICA   1987 pp 198

COUNCIL FOR SCIENTIFIC AND INDUSTRIAL RESEARCH
PRETORIA

This book though mainly covering low-cost buildings for housing, also considers services such as roads, water supply, stormwater, sewerage and electricity distribution.

ACCESS/ROADS/WATER SUPPLY/STORMWATER OPTIONS
/SEWERAGE/ELECTRICITY SUPPLY/SOUTH AFRICA

1109

RECOMMENDED POSITIONS FOR MAINS AND SERVICES
IN NEW STREETS

NATIONAL JOINT UTILITIES GROUP Publication No 7 1984
pp77

NATIONAL JOINT UTILITIES GROUP
LONDON

The distribution of underground services with appropriate depths in any street or pavement is discussed. The recommended order between boundary and kerb being electricity, gas, water then telecommunications nearest the kerb.

SERVICE LOCATION/UK

1110

SHANTY UPGRADING
TECHNICAL HANDBOOK FOR UPGRADING SQUATTER
AND SHANTY SETTLEMENTS

PARRY J.
GORDON A. (editors) 1987 pp86

INTERMEDIATE TECHNOLOGY WORKSHOPS
CRADLEY HEATH

Problems and issues in urban areas are discussed with particular emphasis on finance, affordability and tenure. The role of infrastructure including ground preparation, drainage, roads and access, water supply, power supply, and solid waste is placed within a context of community participation and building for housing.

FINANCE/AFFORDABILITY/GROUND PREPARATION/
DRAINAGE/ROADS/ACCESS/WATER SUPPLY/
SANITATION/UPGRADING/POWER SUPPLY/
COMMUNITY PARTICIPATION/SOLID WASTE

1111

AFFORDABLE HOUSING PROJECTS

ROBERTS M.   1987 p138-208

DEVELOPMENT PLANNING UNIT
BARTLETT SCHOOL OF ARCHITECTURE AND PLANNING
LONDON

A brief introduction to the components of infrastructure with detailed indicative prices for road construction, water supply, sewerage and surface water drainage.

ACCESS/ROAD CONSTRUCTION/WATER SUPPLY/
SANITATION/DRAINAGE/ELECTRICITY SUPPLY/
STREET LIGHTING/SOLID WASTE/COSTS

1112

MANUEL D'URBANISME
VOLUME 5 INFRASTRUCTURE

ROMANN D.
BAEHREL C. 1983 pp393

FRENCH AGENCY FOR OVERSEAS MANAGEMENT AND
DEVELOPMENT
PARIS

In French, this publication contains general data on infrastructure including priorities and constraints. There are technical notes on roads, water supply, public cleansing, sullage and excreta disposal, stormwater, solid waste, electricity supply and street lighting.

WATER SUPPLY/SULLAGE/SANITATION/
STREET LIGHTING/STORM DRAINAGE/SOLID WASTE/
ELECTRICITY SUPPLY/ROADS

1113

A REVIEW OF TECHNOLOGIES FOR THE PROVISION OF
BASIC INFRASTRUCTURE IN LOW-INCOME
SETTLEMENTS

UNCHS HS/40/84/E 1984 pp82

UNITED NATIONS CENTRE FOR HUMAN SETTLEMENTS
NAIROBI

This report describes various technical approaches and examines
social factors which require consideration in planning, installing
and managing infrastructure for low-income communities.

Characteristics of low-income settlements including physical and
infrastructural aspects are investigated along with requirements for
infrastructure in low-income settlements including water supply,
sanitation, solid waste and roads. Institutional and social aspects of
the provision of infrastructure are also considered.

WATER SUPPLY/SANITATION/ROADS/SOLID WASTE/
COSTS/FINANCE

1114

APPROPRIATE INFRASTRUCTURE SERVICES
STANDARDS AND TECHNOLOGIES FOR UPGRADING
SLUM AND SQUATTER AREAS AND RURAL
SETTLEMENTS

UNCHS HS/OP/82-10 1982 pp68

UNITED NATIONS CENTRE FOR HUMAN SETTLEMENTS
NAIROBI

Assessment of available technologies, service levels and standards
for infrastructure in low-income communities. Technologies
assessed include those for new construction and renovation in the
areas of urban water supply, water related sanitation, waterless
sanitation, solid waste disposal drainage and roads and paths.

WATER SUPPLY/SANITATION OPTIONS/
SOLID WASTE/ROADS/DRAINAGE

1201

INCREMENTAL UTILITIES PROVISION AND
AFFORDABILITY

ALLEN D.B.
BLUNT A.C.
FORBES W.D. 1981

IN: WATER, PEOPLE AND WASTE IN DEVELOPING
COUNTRIES
7th WEDC CONFERENCE, MADRAS   p18-23
LOUGHBOROUGH UNIVERSITY OF TECHNOLOGY

The background to and details of the provision of infrastructure in
a settlement in Ismailia, Egypt are outlined. Project objectives
included affordability for the low-income groups involved. The
report includes details of the socio-economic survey which was
conducted, costs of the work and lessons learnt supported by
tabular information.

INFRASTRUCTURE/AFFORDABILITY/COSTS/EGYPT

1202

BEHIND THE TECHNICAL APPROACH TO SLUM
IMPROVEMENT

BAPAT, MEERA
CROOK, NIGEL

WATERLINES VOL 8 NO 1 JULY 1989 p24-26
INTERMEDIATE TECHNOLOGY PUBLICATIONS
LONDON

The author's, based on their work in Pune (western India), argue
that politics and power are as important to health improvement as
taps and toilets. The article also raises the issue of slum
organisation and land management.

INFRASTRUCTURE/INDIA

1203

THE BERTAUD MODEL

BERTAUD M.A.
CARROL A. 1986 pp54

WORLD BANK
WASHINGTON DC

The manual and accompanying micro computer software can assist
planners, designers and decision-makers to investigate the effects
on affordability of: housing density and house construction,
circulation space, differential land pricing, graduated householder
repayments and subsidies.

SITES AND SERVICES/ACCESS/AFFORDABILITY/
LAND PRICING

Infrastructure

1204

URBANISATION PRIMER FOR DESIGN OF
SITES AND SERVICES PROJECTS

CAMINOS H.
GOETHERT R.   1976 pp214

WORLD BANK
WASHINGTON DC

Project assessment is covered including guidelines for
identification and standards, models of evaluation and
demonstration, site analysis and design criteria. Detail including
cost studies is given regarding water supply, sewage disposal
(sewers, septic tanks and aqua privy), circulation, storm drainage,
electricity supply, street lighting, and solid waste disposal.

STANDARDS/WATER SUPPLY/SEWERS/SEPTIC TANKS/
AQUA PRIVY/ROADS/ACCESS/STORM DRAINAGE/
COSTS/ELECTRICITY SUPPLY/SOLID WASTE/
STREET LIGHTING

1205

URBAN INFRASTRUCTURE: TRENDS, NEEDS AND THE
ROLE OF AID

COTTON A.P.
FRANCEYS R.W.A.   1988

HABITAT INTERNATIONAL
VOL 12 (3) pp139-147

A methodology is proposed to achieve sustainability of technical
services through linking technical, financial and social factors by
affordability and willingness to pay. The approach suggested
involves the provision of primary level infrastructure or basic
needs without investment cost recovery but with subsequent
improvements funded through loans to households and
communities.

AFFORDABILITY/UPGRADING/INSTITUTIONS/
COMMUNITY PARTICIPATION

1206

ENGINEERING SERVICES FOR LOW-INCOME HOUSING IN
SRI LANKA

COTTON A.P.
FRANCEYS R.W.A.   1986

Unpublished preprint in
STRATEGIES FOR SLUM AND SQUATTER UPGRADING IN
THE DEVELOPING WORLD
TRIALOG
DARMSTADT

The financial consequences of an incremental approach to
infrastructure provision are investigated based upon the urban
programme of the National Housing Development Authority of Sri
Lanka. Lifecycle costs over a fifteen year period are calculated for
householder and institution for a variety of options.

AFFORDABILITY/COSTS/UPGRADING/
INSTITUTIONS/HOUSEHOLDS/SRI LANKA

1207

URBAN PROJECTS MANUAL
A GUIDE TO PREPARING, UPGRADING AND NEW
DEVELOPMENT PROJECTS ACCESSIBLE TO LOW
INCOME GROUPS

DAVIDSON F.
PAYNE G.   1983. pp148

LIVERPOOL UNIVERSITY PRESS

The manual covers feasibility studies and implementation
including aspects of project location, site development, institutions
and finance. Detail is given on the selection of utility options and
their design supported by technical notes.

WATER SUPPLY/SANITATION/SULLAGE/ROADS/
ELECTRICITY SUPPLY/GROUND PREPARATION/DRAINAGE/
FINANCE

1208

AFFORDABLE URBAN DEVELOPMENT

DAVIDSON F.W.   1981

PLANNING AND DEVELOPMENT IN DEVELOPING
COUNTRIES
PROCEEDINGS OF SEMINAR F
UNIVERSITY OF WARWICK   p119-126
PTRC EDUCATION AND RESEARCH SERVICES

This paper highlights the problems in defining affordability. It
proposes alternative design approaches to minimise the problems
of design within defined limits. A case study from Ismailia Egypt
is used for illustration.

INFRASTRUCTURE/AFFORDABILITY/EGYPT

1209

CASE STUDIES IN DEVELOPMENT ADMINISTRATION
VOL 2: URBAN SERVICES

DAVIES C.J. 1976 pp129

DEVELOPMENT ADMINISTRATION GROUP
UNIVERSITY OF BIRMINGHAM

Infrastructure

Topics covered include the provision and management of housing, resettlement of squatters, urban redevelopment, sewerage and sewage disposal and solid waste disposal. Management and operation of sewerage and sewage disposal systems are outlined in more detail.

SEWERAGE/SOLID WASTE/COSTS/MANAGEMENT/
OPERATION

1210

FINANCING OF SQUATTER AREA UPGRADING
PROGRAMMES

DEVAS N.   1982

PLANNING AND DEVELOPMENT IN DEVELOPING
COUNTRIES

PROCEEDINGS OF SEMINAR F
UNIVERSITY OF WARWICK   p35-48
PTRC EDUCATION AND RESEARCH SERVICES

Alternative approaches to financing are outlined including self help, full cost recovery and government provision. Principal sources of finance for upgrading are discussed together with the opportunities for mobilising these resources, and options for repayment.

INFRASTRUCTURE/FINANCE/COST RECOVERY/
COMMUNITY PARTICIPATION

1211

THE ENGINEER IN AN UNDERPRIVILEGED
ENVIRONMENT

FOSTER R.
CROSSLEY T.R.   1980

WATER AND WASTE ENGINEERING IN AFRICA
6th WEDC CONFERENCE NIGERIA   p45-48
LOUGHBOROUGH UNIVERSITY OF TECHNOLOGY

The report describes upgrading of low-income housing areas in five cities in Ghana. A brief description of the study sites is given, including administration, finance, maintenance, provision of facilities, community involvement and cost recovery.

INFRASTRUCTURE/UPGRADING/COST RECOVERY/
COMMUNITY PARTICIPATION/GHANA

1212

BENEFITS AND SUSTAINABILITY IN INFRASTRUCTURE
PROVISION: INDIA AND SRI LANKA

FRANCEYS RICHARD
COTTON ANDREW

Unpublished preprint
EMERGING TRENDS IN THIRD WORLD HOUSING
POLICIES
CDPS
UNIVERSITY OF SHEFFIELD
6TH INTER SCHOOLS CONFERENCE ON DEVELOPMENT
18-19 MARCH 1989

The paper focuses on the provision of sustainable, affordable infrastructure that is necessary to support low-income urban housing programmes. Based on work developed in India and Sri Lanka, the paper examines ways of involving communities and householders in the planning selection and design of least cost infrastructure which has the potential to be incrementally upgraded according to the time schedule and desires of the people.

INFRASTRUCTURE/BENEFITS/COSTS/UPGRADING/
COMMUNITY PARTICIPATION/INDIA/SRI LANKA

1213

SITES AND SERVICES

GOETHERT R. 1985

ARCHITECTURAL REVIEW VOL 178 1985 8/p 28-81
THE ARCHITECTURAL PRESS   LONDON

A review of the state of sites and services approach and trends in current practice with analysis of the advantages and problems. Infrastructure layout plans are described together with a discussion of the role of architects.

INFRASTRUCTURE/SITES AND SERVICES

1214

SHELTER, INFRASTRUCTURE AND SERVICES IN THIRD
WORLD CITIES

HARDOY JORGE E.
SATTERTHWAITE DAVID

HABITAT INTERNATIONAL, VOL 10, NO 3, p245-284, 1986

The paper, divided into 6 sections, discusses the nature of housing need among 'the poor', the ways used for finding accommodation and the ways cities are being built. It also assesses the effectiveness of public housing programmes, outlines more effective approaches and drawing on these experiences, suggests a more effective approach to the mounting problems in Third World cities.

INFRASTRUCTURE

1215

SQUATTER, SELF BUILDERS AND SUPPORTS

KELLET P.
KONCKE C.   1987

OPEN HOUSE INTERNATIONAL VOL 12 (4) p 55-63
SCHOOL OF ARCHITECTURE
UNIVERSITY OF NEWCASTLE UPON TYNE

This paper investigates how the efforts of self help builders can be
maximised. It identifies the aspects that are best left to the
participants and those that require external input. A case study is
described involving consolidation of the settlement and space
reorganisation at settlement and dwelling level.

INFRASTRUCTURE/COMMUNITY PARTICIPATION/
COLOMBIA

1216

SELF HELP AND SHELTER RELATED
PROGRAMMES IN LIBERIA

LACEY L.
OWUSU S.E.   1987

JOURNAL OF THE AMERICAN PLANNING ASSOCIATION
VOL 53 (2)   p206-212
AMERICAN PLANNING ASSOCIATION

This article investigates self help strategies for community
upgrading including shelter, in sites and services and community
projects in Liberia.

INFRASTRUCTURE/SITES AND SERVICES/
COMMUNITY PARTICIPATION/LIBERIA

1217

BASIC HOUSING: POLICIES FOR URBAN SITES, SERVICES
AND SHELTER IN DEVELOPING COUNTRIES

LAQUIAN A.A.   1983   pp163

IDRC REPORT 208E
OTTAWA

Although the monograph is primarily about actual experiences in
the formulation and implementation of basic housing policies, it
compares the costs of infrastructure in sites and services
programmes with regard to potential affordability and cost
recovery mechanisms.

SITES AND SERVICES/AFFORDABILITY/
COSTS/COMMUNITY PARTICIPATION

1218

COMMUNITY PARTICIPATION IN PROJECT
PLANNING AND IMPLEMENTATION

LEVE G.   1984

WATER AND SANITATION IN ASIA AND THE PACIFIC
10th WEDC CONFERENCE SINGAPORE p75-78
LOUGHBOROUGH UNIVERSITY OF TECHNOLOGY

Using a case study from the Solomon Islands strategies to involve
the community in changing their own customs and habits are
examined.

INFRASTRUCTURE/COMMUNITY PARTICIPATION/
SOLOMON ISLANDS

1219

THE SITES AND SERVICES APPROACH REVIEWED:
SOLUTION OR STOPGAP TO THE THIRD WORLD
HOUSING SHORTAGE

LINDEN van der J. 1986 pp178

GOWER PUBLISHING CO LTD
ALDERSHOT

Comprises a review of the work of many authors on sites and
services schemes with the emphasis on housing, affordability and
cost recovery. The costs of imposing too high standards for
housing and services is recognised as significant in reducing the
benefits to the poorest.

SITES AND SERVICES/AFFORDABILITY

1220

SITES AND SERVICES APPROACH FOR HOUSING LOW
INCOME FAMILIES

MENEZES L.
MYERS M
SIVARAMAKRISHNAN K.C.   1979

COURSE NOTES 770/1003 CN-208
ECONOMIC DEVELOPMENT INSTITUTE
WORLD BANK WASHINGTON DC

These notes outline the rationale and operational issues of the sites
and services approach of low-income housing. Items include site
selection, target population, implementation, standards, cost
recovery. Together with examples from El Salvador, Tanzania and
India, tabulated information is presented from urbanisation
projects throughout the world.

SITES AND SERVICES/COST RECOVERY/EL SALVADOR/
TANZANIA/INDIA

1221

UPGRADING OF SLUMS

MENEZES L.
MYERS M
SIVARAMAKRISHNAN K.C.   1979

COURSE NOTES 775/003 CN 209
ECONOMIC DEVELOPMENT INSTITUTE
WORLD BANK
WASHINGTON DC

These notes outline the rationale and operational issues of slum upgrading. Items include - criteria for selection, land tenure, community participation, and cost recovery. Examples are presented from programmes in Indonesian Kampungs, Peru and Zambia.

INFRASTRUCTURE/UPGRADING/
COMMUNITY PARTICIPATION/COSTS/
INDONESIA/PERU/ZAMBIA

1222

LOW INCOME HOUSING IN THE DEVELOPING WORLD
THE ROLE OF SITES AND SERVICES AND SETTLEMENT
UPGRADING

PAYNE G.K. ed.   1984 pp271

JOHN WILEY AND SONS
CHICHESTER

A comprehensive review of experience in sites and services and site upgrading schemes. It includes a review of projects in various countries and discusses political and administrative factors, the role of international agencies and consultants, community participation in housing and finance and affordability. Land issues, the provision of infrastructure and utility services and alternative building materials and construction systems are also covered.

SITES AND SERVICES/COMMUNITY PARTICIPATION/
FINANCE/UPGRADING/AFFORDABILITY

1223

REACHING THE TARGET GROUP

PELTENBURG M.
LINDEN van der J.   1987

OPEN HOUSE INTERNATIONAL VOL 12 NO 4   p74-76
SCHOOL OF ARCHITECTURE
UNIVERSITY OF NEWCASTLE UPON TYNE

Implementation of a housing scheme in Pakistan using an incremental scheme to overcome the problems of delayed inhabitation.

INFRASTRUCTURE/IMPLEMENTATION/PAKISTAN

1224

ENVIRONMENTAL IMPROVEMENT IN SLUMS THROUGH
COMMUNITY PARTICIPATION

RAMAMURTHY K.N.
THOMAS P.R. 1984

WATER AND SANITATION IN ASIA AND THE PACIFIC
10th WEDC CONFERENCE SINGAPORE p83-86
LOUGHBOROUGH UNIVERSITY OF TECHNOLOGY

Characteristics of slums and squatter settlements are described together with community participation in their improvement. A case study of Madras city is given with detail on the growth and evolution of slums, and the slum upgrading programme which has been followed.

INFRASTRUCTURE/COMMUNITY PARTICIPATION/
UPGRADING/INDIA

1225

BETWEEN BASTI DWELLERS AND BUREAUCRATS

SCHOORL J.W.
LINDEN van der J.J
YAP K.S.   1983   pp305

PERGAMON PRESS
OXFORD

Squatter settlement upgrading in Karachi including history, housing policy, financing, implementation, planning, and community participation.

INFRASTRUCTURE/UPGRADING/FINANCE/
COMMUNITY PARTICIPATION/PAKISTAN

1226

THIRD WORLD URBAN HOUSING

SHANKLAND COX PARTNERSHIP 1977

BUILDING RESEARCH ESTABLISHMENT
WATFORD

Project upgrading as covered in Chapter 11 includes general principles, selecting priority areas, standards , implementation procedures and community participation. Chapter 12 on sites and services encompasses planning, community participation, implementation, finance, construction and supervision and costs.

INFRASTRUCTURE/COMMUNITY PARTICIPATION/
FINANCE/COSTS/UPGRADING

Infrastructure

1227

DENSITIES IN HOUSING AREAS
TROPICAL BUILDING STUDIES No 1

STEVENS P.H.M.   1960

HMSO CODE NO 47-215-1 pp 55
LONDON

The significance of housing density is analysed to aid decision
making. The relationship of density to technical services is
investigated for single and multi-storey buildings.

HOUSING DENSITY/SERVICES

1228

REVIEW OF THE PROVISION OF INFRASTRUCTURE IN
SLUMS AND SQUATTER AREAS AND RURAL
SETTLEMENTS

UNCHS CHS/OP/81/5 1981 pp48

UNITED NATIONS CENTRE FOR HUMAN SETTLEMENTS
NAIROBI

This review of the infrastructure problems in developing countries
outlines the scope and dimension of the problem. Current
approaches to the provision of infrastructure are presented
together with conclusions and recommendations for future
intervention. A summary of the level of water and sanitation
provision throughout the world is included.

INFRASTRUCTURE/WATER SUPPLY/SANITATION

1229

SITES AND SERVICES SCHEMES
THE SCOPE FOR COMMUNITY PARTICIPATION

UNCHS TRAINING SERIES 1984 pp44
HS/38/84/E

UNITED NATIONS CENTRE FOR HUMAN SETTLEMENTS
NAIROBI

Community participation in sites and services schemes is
discussed with descriptions of responsibilities for each phase of
development. Formulation of criteria, recruitment of beneficiaries,
planning the settlement, project and plot development financing
are all outlined together with the design   and construction of the
dwellings.

COMMUNITY PARTICIPATION/SITES AND SERVICES

1230

DELIVERY OF BASIC INFRASTRUCTURE TO LOW
INCOME SETTLEMENTS. ISSUES AND OPTIONS

UNCHS 1986 pp34
HS/101/86/E

UNITED NATIONS CENTRE FOR HUMAN SETTLEMENTS
NAIROBI

This overview of the current status of basic infrastructure includes
sections on water supply, sanitation, drainage and solid waste in
developing countries. Attempts are made to identify the constraints
in delivery of services together with discussion of the scope and
dimensions of the problems. Technological, institutional and
financial factors which influence the provision of infrastructure are
also explored.

INFRASTRUCTURE/WATER SUPPLY/SANITATION/
DRAINAGE/SOLID WASTE/OPERATION/MAINTENANCE/
FINANCE/COST RECOVERY

1231

COMMUNITY PARTICIPATION IN SQUATTER
SETTLEMENT UPGRADING

UNCHS TRAINING SERIES 1985 pp44
HS/69/84

UNITED NATIONS CENTRE FOR HUMAN SETTLEMENTS
NAIROBI

Community participation in squatter settlement upgrading is
described in this training publication. Sections are included on
selection and survey of settlements, community organisations,
planning, financing, implementation, charges, house construction
and improvements.

INFRASTRUCTURE/COMMUNITY PARTICIPATION/
SQUATTER SETTLEMENTS

1232

UPGRADING OF URBAN SLUMS AND SQUATTER AREAS

UNCHS CHS/OP/81/4 1981 pp39

UNITED NATIONS CENTRE FOR HUMAN SETTLEMENTS
NAIROBI

This paper summarises the situation in urban slums and squatter
settlements and government responses to the unresolved problems,
with a view to making recommendations to governments and
international organisations. The need for upgrading is examined
from a policy perspective including a review of existing criteria.
The major issues of affordability and cost recovery are also
examined.

INFRASTRUCTURE/AFFORDABILITY/COST RECOVERY

1233

PHYSICAL IMPROVEMENT OF SLUM & SQUATTER
SETTLEMENTS

REPORT OF AN EXPERT GROUP MEETING IN
NASSAU, BAHAMAS 1977
UNCHS CHS/R/80 - 1/S 1980 pp98

UNITED NATIONS CENTRE FOR HUMAN SETTLEMENTS
NAIROBI

The report, beginning with an introduction to slum formation
outlines existing policy, including government attitudes and
considerations, with regard to the selection of improvements.
Existing situations are described including site conditions, land
use and population densities as well as infrastructural issues
relating to water supply, solid waste, power supply and sanitation.

INFRASTRUCTURE/WATER SUPPLY/SOLID WASTE/
POWER SUPPLY/SANITATION/ROADS/UPGRADING

1234

PARTICIPATION IN URBAN DEVELOPMENT

URBAN EDGE VOL 8 (5) 1984 p1-8

WORLD BANK
WASHINGTON DC

General notes on the obstacles to and control of community
participation are given with illustration from three country studies
in El Salvador, Botswana and Nicaragua.

COMMUNITY PARTICIPATION/DEVELOPMENT/
EL SALVADOR/BOTSWANA/NICARAGUA

1235

COMMUNITY LEADERSHIP AND SELF HELP HOUSING

WARD P.
CHANT S.   1987

PROGRESS IN PLANNING VOL 27 (2) p73-133

PERGAMON JOURNALS LTD
OXFORD

Findings based on a thorough review of experience throughout the
Third World on the aspects of leadership in a community and its
influence on the processes of urban development.

It includes sections on the nature of community leadership,
decision making in low-income settlements, the emergence of
leaders, their impact upon community development and strategies
for reaching the poor through leaders.

SERVICES/COMMUNITY PARTICIPATION/DEVELOPMENT

1236

INHABITANT PARTICIPATION IN THE PROCESS OF
SQUATTER UPGRADING WITH SPECIAL REGARD TO THE
TECHNICAL INFRASTRUCTURE

WEHENPOHL G.   1986

Unpublished preprint in
STRATEGIES FOR SLUM AND SQUATTER UPGRADING IN
THE DEVELOPING WORLD BERLIN 27-29 NOVEMBER
1986
TRIALOG
DARMSTADT

This paper, giving definitions of self help describes the capabilities
and the limitations of self help schemes. A case study of Brazilian
favelas includes descriptions of the existing situation, supply of
infrastructure and the role of institutions in influencing self help at
different stages in the project.

INFRASTRUCTURE/ROADS/WATER SUPPLY/SOLID WASTE
/STORM DRAINAGE/COMMUNITY PARTICIPATION/
BRAZIL

1237

ANALYSIS OF DESIGN ALTERNATIVES FOR
EVOLUTIONARY SETTLEMENTS

WILLIAMSON G   1982

BIE BULLETIN REF No 11 p109-
WEENA, ROTTERDAM

A series of models for planning and development of housing
settlements are presented which depend upon community
participation as the basic resource. The study analyses and
evaluates the various factors involved in design decisions for
housing programmes which are evolutionary in nature, including
the provision of site infrastructure.

HOUSING DENSITY/LAYOUT/SERVICES/
COMMUNITY PARTICIPATION

1238

SITES AND SERVICES

A WORLD BANK PAPER 1974   pp47

WORLD BANK
WASHINGTON DC

A paper detailing the principles of Sites and Service projects. Topic areas covered include project design (design population, scope of sites and services, design standards and site location) project financing (cost, charges and subsidies) and project organisation (management, selection of settlers, legal aspects, and community participation). Methodologies outlined include cost/benefit analysis and the evaluation of upgrading programmes.

SITES AND SERVICES/FINANCE/COSTS/
UPGRADING/COMMUNITY PARTICIPATION

1301

BARRIERS TO RESIDENT PARTICIPATION IN SLUM IMPROVEMENT: THE MAINTENANCE QUESTION.

COTTON A.P.
SKINNER R.J.   1990

COMMUNITY DEVELOPMENT JOURNAL VOL 25 NO 1
OXFORD UNIVERSITY PRESS p37-41

The technical issues involved with maintenance of infrastructure in slum improvement projects in Hyderabad, India are described in relationship to the community development approach. The difficulties in enabling community participation in maintenance are ascribed to problems in involving communities in crucial planning decisions and in the choice of technology adapted for infrastructure.

COMMUNITY PARTICIPATION/MAINTENANCE/INDIA

1302

SERVICES BY A SUPPORT APPROACH -
INFRASTRUCTURE FOR URBAN HOUSING IN SRI LANKA

COTTON A.P.
FRANCEYS R.W.A.   1988

OPEN HOUSE INTERNATIONAL VOL 13 NO 4 p43-48
SCHOOL OF ARCHITECTURE
UNIVERSITY OF NEWCASTLE UPON TYNE

Technical options for infrastructure with respect to Sri Lanka are described along with lifecycle costings for possible upgrading routes.

INFRASTRUCTURE/COSTS/SRI LANKA

1303

OPERATION AND MAINTENANCE OF SERVICES FOR URBAN LOW INCOME HOUSING IN SRI LANKA

GUNASEKERA S.G.V.D.H.   1987

Unpublished MSc thesis pp158

LOUGHBOROUGH UNIVERSITY OF TECHNOLOGY

This thesis gives a guide to appropriate operation and maintenance procedures and discusses provision and responsibility. In addition to background information on the area are sections on government and involved organisations, operation and maintenance services in Colombo, finance, and existing operation and maintenance programmes with reference to a local case study.

INFRASTRUCTURE/OPERATION/MAINTENANCE/
FINANCE/SRI LANKA

1304

THE ROLE OF COMMUNITY DEVELOPMENT IN A SLUM IMPROVEMENT PROJECT

MARSDEN D.   1988

MANCHESTER PAPERS ON DEVELOPMENT VOL 4 NO 2
P159-188

The background and historical development of policy approaches to slum improvement in Hyderabad, India are described. Attention is focussed on the problems of relationships between the different departments of local government involved and on the areas of tension which develop in an expanding programme of slum improvement.

COMMUNITY PARTICIPATION/
PROGRAMME DEVELOPMENT/INDIA

1305

MAINTENANCE: A DEVELOPMENT PRIORITY

URBAN EDGE VOL 10 NO 3 1986 pp8

WORLD BANK
WASHINGTON DC

A general outline of the problems of maintaining existing facilities together with possible solutions is given. Programmes of improved city maintenance in the Philippines, Sri Lanka and Ghana are described together with suggestions on the design of a maintenance system.

SERVICES/MAINTENANCE/PHILIPPINES/SRI LANKA/
GHANA

1306

URBAN PROJECT DEVELOPMENT TRENDS - PHILIPPINES

WRAY A. 1988

WATER AND URBAN SERVICES IN ASIA AND THE
PACIFIC ppi-iii p1-158
14th WEDC CONFERENCE KUALA LUMPUR

LOUGHBOROUGH UNIVERSITY OF TECHNOLOGY

A review of urban development projects undertaken in the
Phillipines in terms of objectives, components and implementation
experience that suggests approaches that may be considered to
support infrastructure provision amidst rapid urbanisation.

SERVICES/IMPLEMENTATION/PHILLIPINES

1401

EVALUATION OF SITES AND SERVICES PROJECTS. THE
EXPERIENCE FROM LUSAKA, ZAMBIA.

BAMBERGER M.   1982
SANYAUB
VALVERDE, N

WORLD BANK STAFF WORKING PAPER 548   pp203
WORLD BANK
WASHINGTON DC

This report presents the findings of a five year evaluation of the
first Lusaka Sites and Services project. The report includes
sections on project scope, design and organisation, financing and
operating efficiency. Standards for infrastructure are included.

SITES AND SERVICES/FINANCE/OPERATION/ZAMBIA

1402

EVALUATION OF SITES AND SERVICES PROJECTS. THE
EVIDENCE FROM EL SALVADOR

BAMBERGER M.
GONZALEZ-POLIO E.
SAE-HAU U.   1982

WORLD BANK STAFF WORKING PAPER 549   pp286
WORLD BANK
WASHINGTON DC

A five year evaluation of the effectiveness of the first El Salvador
Sites and Services project is described with emphasis on the
accessibility to services. Evaluation also considers the extent of
cost recovery achieved and the
adequacy of the design.

SITES AND SERVICES/COST RECOVERY/EL SALVADOR

1403

ENVIRONMENTAL PLANNING OF BUSTEE AREAS IN
CALCUTTA METROPOLITAN DISTRICT

BANERJEE M.
MUKHERJEE S.K.   1982

WATER AND WASTE ENGINEERING IN ASIA
8th WEDC CONFERENCE MADRAS   p1, p130-133
LOUGHBOROUGH UNIVERSITY OF TECHNOLOGY

A short description of existing and proposed facilities is given,
including costs and standards for such services as water supply,
latrines, drainage, garbage collection, pathways and street
lighting.

INFRASTRUCTURE/COSTS/INDIA

1404

THE MORPHOLOGY OF INFORMAL SETTLEMENTS INDIA

BAREVIN C.
BHATT V.C.
BROOK R.
PURI R.
RYBCZYNSKI W. (undated)

CENTRE FOR MINIMUM COST HOUSING pp38
McGILL UNIVERSITY
MONTREAL

This paper puts forward the view that the shelter needs of the
people are constricted within a set of locally specific socio-
economic constraints. The basic physical aspects such as plot area,
frontage and available space are analysed.

PLOT SIZE/LAYOUT/ACCESS/SPACE/INDIA

1405

THE DELHI SITES AND SERVICES EXPERIENCE: A BRIEF
HISTORY

BHATT V.C.   1988

OPEN HOUSE INTERNATIONAL VOL 13 NO 1   p43-46
SCHOOL OF ARCHITECTURE
UNIVERSITY OF NEWCASTLE UPON TYNE

A brief history of the Sites and Services approach in Delhi is given
including the discussion of the reduction of standards of
infrastructure to more affordable limits and planning infrastructure
implemented during the emergency years.

SITES AND SERVICES/AFFORDABILITY/INDIA

1406

REPORT ON MABOTE SITES AND SERVICES SCHEME

BINNIE CONSULTANTS   1985

BINNIE AND PARTNERS
Unpublished report for
Government of Lesotho Ministry of the Interior

The report comprises a feasibility study into pre-serviced sites in Lesotho. Volume 2 contains background information into the site, planning of the site and evaluation of alternative options for development. Proposals on the structure of the project are made covering physical infrastructure, financing, economic   analysis and implementation. Volume 3 comprises appendices including engineering studies (water supply, sanitation, roads, drainage, electricity supply, solid waste), engineering design criteria, and data used for the cost estimates, such as shadow prices and costs of the components of the infrastructure.

INFRASTRUCTURE/COST RECOVERY/IMPLEMENTATION/ LESOTHO

1407

SQUATTER AREA IMPROVEMENTS
NAM SHAN MEI UPPER VILLAGE PRELIMINARY REPORT
HONG KONG

BINNIE CONSULTANTS   1987

BINNIE AND PARTNERS pi, 1-3
HONG KONG

The report outlines the location and topography of the area together with recommendations for improvements of services such as surface water drains, street lighting, water distribution, footpath and access upgrading, and solid waste collection. Included is a design for an aqua privy toilet block.

SURFACE DRAINS/STREET LIGHTING/WATER SUPPLY/
FOOTPATHS/ACCESS/UPGRADING/SOLID WASTE/
AQUA PRIVY/HONG KONG

1408

AN ANALYSIS OF SQUATTER RESETTLEMENT
PROGRAMMES IN BANGLADESH

CHOGUILL C.   1980

URBAN AND REGIONAL PLANNING IN DEVELOPING
COUNTRIES
PROCEEDINGS OF SEMINAR H
UNIVERSITY OF WARWICK   p73-82
PTRC EDUCATION AND RESEARCH SERVICES

An introduction and background to squatter settlement programmes in Bangladesh is given. The Mirpur/Bashantek project which includes embankment construction and pumping facilities for stormwater control is outlined together with details of the problems in organisation, technology and resources.

INFRASTRUCTURE/STORMWATER OPTIONS/BANGLADESH

1409

PROPOSED MEASURES FOR REDUCING COSTS IN
INFRASTRUCTURE AND URBANISATION PROJECTS FOR
LOW INCOME HOUSING IN HONDURAS

CORDON R.O.   1982

WASH FIELD REPORT NO 46   pp71
WATER AND SANITATION FOR HEALTH
VIRGINIA, USA

The report comprises a cost analysis of water and waste disposal systems projects in Honduras with considerations of institutional effects on costs and measures to solve these. Some background to the project is also given. System capital costs are tabulated.

INFRASTRUCTURE/WATER SUPPLY/
WASTE WATER DISPOSAL/COSTS/HONDURAS

1410

SERVICES FOR URBAN LOW-INCOME HOUSING

COTTON A.P.
FRANCEYS R.W.A.   (UNDATED) pp75

NHDA, SRI LANKA AND
WATER ENGINEERING AND DEVELOPMENT CENTRE
LOUGHBOROUGH UNIVERSITY OF TECHNOLOGY

The guidelines contain information for planning and design of the technical services for low-income housing. The main sections relate to ground preparation, drainage roads and access, water supply, sanitation, solid waste, and power supply. Other topics include upgrading and community participation, all related to work carried out by the National Housing Development Authority, Sri Lanka.

INFRASTRUCTURE/UPGRADING/
COMMUNITY PARTICIPATION/SRI LANKA

1411

SERVICES FOR URBAN LOW INCOME HOUSING

COTTON A.P.
FRANCEYS R.W.A.   1988

WATER AND URBAN SERVICES IN ASIA AND THE
PACIFIC
14th WEDC CONFERENCE KUALA LUMPUR p115-119
LOUGHBOROUGH UNIVERSITY OF TECHNOLOGY

A description of the project in Galle in southern Sri Lanka and proposals for a model for sustained urban services is given. Different approaches to the provision of services including incremental improvement and infrastructure for the Million House programme are discussed.

SERVICES/IMPLEMENTATION/SRI LANKA

1412

CASE STUDIES OF SITE AND SERVICE SCHEMES IN
KENYA

de KRUIJFF G.J.
CHANA T.S.   1980   pp165

HOUSING RESEARCH AND DEVELOPMENT UNIT
UNIVERSITY OF NAIROBI

Sites and services programmes in Kenya are outlined giving their
historical background and present situation. An evaluation of the
programmes is made with inventories of each of the schemes. Case
studies presented include information on site area and location,
public utilities, user costs, site development and site observations.

SITES AND SERVICES/COSTS/KENYA

1413

GALLE URBAN PROJECT MANUAL 2

DPU/NHDA/WEDC   1987

DEVELOPMENT PLANNING UNIT
BARTLETT SCHOOL OF ARCHITECTURE AND PLANNING
LONDON

This programme overview including the operating principles of the
infrastructure services describes the role of the development
councils, sources of financial assistance in addition to the costs and
standards of the infrastructure. Appendices include layouts of
plots, infrastructure costs and details of the electricity supply.

INFRASTRUCTURE/FINANCE/COSTS/
ELECTRICITY SUPPLY/SRI LANKA

1414

ENGINEERING DESIGN STANDARDS AND GUIDELINES
METRO MANILA. MINISTRY OF PUBLIC WORKS.
INFRASTRUCTURE UTILITIES AND ENGINEERING
PROGRAM

GILMORE HANKEY KIRKE   1981

GILMORE HANKEY KIRKE
LONDON

This manual includes criteria for the design and construction of the
piped water supply, (including pipelines, standposts, storage, and
elevated tanks), wells (deep and shallow), sanitation (communal
facilities), drainage (pipes and canals) and street improvements.

INFRASTRUCTURE/WATER SUPPLY/PIPES/STANDPOST/
WATER TANKS/WELLS/SANITATION/
COMMUNAL LATRINES/OPERATION/MAINTENANCE/
CANALS/ROADS/DRAINAGE/PHILIPPINES

1415

URBAN DEVELOPMENT PROJECT APPRAISAL MISSION -
YEMEN ARAB REPUBLIC

GILMORE HANKEY KIRKE
WRAY A.G.   1981

Unpublished report for
URBAN PROJECTS DIVISION, WORLD BANK

The project terms of reference and programme of work are
described together with details of the sites including proposed
infrastructure, proposed operation and maintenance and project
implementation. Included are annexes on the existing situation of
the sites, details of proposed levels of infrastructure, cost data and
solid waste and street cleansing options.

INFRASTRUCTURE/OPERATION/MAINTENANCE COSTS/
YEMEN

1416

PROJET DE DEVELOPPEMENT URBAIN: YAOUNDE
DOUALA

HALCROW FOX AND ASSOCIATES   1980 p1-28

MINISTERE DE L'URBANISME ET DE L'HABITAT
CAMEROUN

In the context of planning the upgrading of urban settlements in
Yaounde and Douala this consultant's report in French, examines
access requirements and costs of drainage, water supply and
electricity supply.

ACCESS/COSTS

1417

"MANE" AN INITIATIVE IN PUBLIC HOUSING

HUDCO 1987 pp136

HUDCO/SANDEEPRINTS PUBLICATION
NEW DELHI

Case studies of sites and services schemes in India. Each case
study details briefly the site, soil conditions, and services - water
supply, sanitation, solid waste, drainage, roads and electricity
supply which were adopted in the programme.

WATER SUPPLY/SANITATION/SOLID WASTE/DRAINAGE/
ROADS/ELECTRICITY SUPPLY/INDIA

1418

SITES AND SERVICES PROJECTS IN THE THIRD WORLD

JAYASEKERA N.G.   1988 pp314

Unpublished BSc thesis
LOUGHBOROUGH UNIVERSITY OF TECHNOLOGY

A comparison between two Sites and Services projects, one in Sri
Lanka and the other in the Philippines. The report discusses the
options available for infrastructure and those adopted in each of
the countries. A comparison of cost is included and the Bertaud
model was used to establish the affordability of the project to the
initiating agency. The components of infrastructure covered
include water supply, sanitation, solid waste, access, drainage,
power, and roads.

INFRASTRUCTURE/COSTS/PHILIPPINES/SRI LANKA

1419

THE REHABILITATION PROGRAMME OF ALAGADOS
SQUATTER SETTLEMENT IN BRAZIL

MATHEY K.   1978

EKISTICS VOL 45 (27,0)   p257-261
ATHENS CENTRE OF EKISTICS

An evaluation of the squatter settlement is presented, including
infrastructure costs, as compared with the aims and conditions of
the rehabilitation programme.

SERVICES/COSTS/SQUATTER SETTLEMENTS/BRAZIL

1420

ISMAILIA DEMONSTRATION PROJECT EGYPT
VOL 3 (TECHNICAL)

ODA 1978 pp180

OVERSEAS DEVELOPMENT ADMINISTRATION
LONDON

Final report on a demonstration project in Egypt with sections on
the background to the area, transport and roads - including
standards and technical details and parameters in each
infrastructure sector. Detail on costs, affordability and the various
financing institutions involved is included.

INFRASTRUCTURE/AFFORDABILITY/COSTS/FINANCE/
EGYPT

1421

VISAKHAPATNAM SLUM IMPROVEMENT PROJECT WITH
ODA ASSISTANCE

CHILAKAPETA SLUM, HYDERABAD INDIA

ODA   1988 pp24

OVERSEAS DEVELOPMENT ADMINISTRATION
LONDON

A brief history of the slum is given together with a socio-economic
profile and an outline of existing and proposed facilities which
include drainage, roads, and communal latrines.

INDIA/DRAINAGE/COMMUNAL LATRINES/ROADS

1422

VISAKHAPATNAM SLUM IMPROVEMENT PROJECT WITH
ODA ASSISTANCE

INDIRA NAGAR-1 SLUM
VISAKHAPATNAM HYDERABAD INDIA

REGIONAL CENTRE FOR URBAN AND ENVIRONMENTAL
STUDIES, HYDERABAD AND
DEVELOPMENT PLANNING UNIT, LONDON

A brief history of the project is given, including the existing and
proposed infrastructure for drainage, roads and water supply. A
bill of quantities and costs are included.

DRAINAGE/ROADS/WATER SUPPLY/COSTS/INDIA

1423

INDIAN HUMAN SETTLEMENTS PROGRAMME
RESEARCH REPORT 5
APPROPRIATE TECHNICAL DESIGN
LOW INCOME SETTLEMENT INFRASTRUCTURE

ROY S.K.
DUTTA P.K.
ROY K.   1988   pp190

HUMAN SETTLEMENT MANAGEMENT INSTITUTE
NEW DELHI

The report outlines the study findings and recommendations, as
well as providing an introduction to urban settlements in India and
their infrastructure. The study objectives are outlined and a
summary of relevant literature on infrastructure presented covering
drainage, sanitation, solid waste and water supply.

INFRASTRUCTURE/INDIA

1424

SLUM UPGRADING IN VISAKHAPATAM (INDIA)

SARMA Bh.V.   1986

Unpublished preprint in
STRATEGIES FOR SLUM AND SQUATTER UPGRADING IN
THE DEVELOPING WORLD pp19
TRIALOG
DARMSTADT

This critical study of slum upgrading describes three slum schemes
where environmentalf improvement schemes have been
implemented. The facilities provided are described and their
performance evaluated with recommendations presented.

UPGRADING/STANDPOSTS/SULLAGE/DRAINAGE/ROADS/
COMMUNAL LATRINES/STREET LIGHTING/INDIA

1425

SITES AND SERVICES PROJECTS IN TANZANIA

SIEBOLDS P.
STEINBERG F. 1982

HABITAT INTERNATIONAL VOL 6 1/2   p109-130
PERGAMON PRESS
OXFORD

This case study of implementation under the Second National
Sites and Services project includes analysis of the problems of
implementation. Sections in the report include implementation,
site selection and preparation, and community participation.

SITES AND SERVICES/IMPLEMENTATION/COST/
TANZANIA

1426

UPGRADING OF BASTI SAIDAN SHAH

SIKANDER S. 1982

WATER AND WASTE ENGINEERING IN ASIA
8th WEDC CONFERENCE MADRAS   p126-129
LOUGHBOROUGH UNIVERSITY OF TECHNOLOGY

Characteristics of a slum in Lahore including economic housing
and environmental aspects are described together with upgrading
policy for water supply, drainage and sewerage and options for
cost recovery.

SERVICES/WATER SUPPLY/DRAINAGE/SEWERS/
COST RECOVERY/PAKISTAN

1427

INTEGRAL UPGRADING PLAN FOR MARGINAL
SETTLEMENTS IN MANAGUA: OBSERVATIONS ON
ASPECTS OF TECHNOLOGY

SILVA R.T.   1986 pp16

Unpublished preprint in
STRATEGIES FOR SLUM AND SQUATTER UPGRADING IN
THE DEVELOPING WORLD
TRIALOG
DARMSTADT

A review of the present situation with regard to water supply,
sullage, drainage, solid waste, and roads is given and various
technological options are described in the upgrading program
proposed for two barrios. Specific technological alternatives for
sewage and solid residue collection are detailed in an annex.

SERVICES/UPGRADING/WATER SUPPLY/SULLAGE/
ROADS/SOLID WASTE/NICARAGUA

1428

A SITES AND SERVICE AND AREA UPGRADING PROJECT
IN UPPER VOLTA

UNDESA   1978

EKISTICS VOL 45 (270)   p262-267
ATHENS CENTRE OF EKISTICS

A review of the aspects involved in sites and services and site
upgrading projects in Upper Volta. Included are sections on
planning and implementation, selection of participants, building
standards, financing participation as well as a comparison between
sites and services and upgrading plot sizes.

SITES AND SERVICES/IMPLEMENTATION/UPPER VOLTA

1429

INFRASTRUCTURE DEVELOPMENT ANALYSIS FOR LOW
INCOME HOUSING AT SUMMITPURA

WICKRAMASENA A.K.A.   1986 pp35

Unpublished research report
WATER ENGINEERING AND DEVELOPMENT CENTRE
LOUGHBOROUGH UNIVERSITY OF TECHNOLOGY

The report describes the present status of the project and includes
sections on options for ground preparation, options for sanitation
(including leaching tanks, communal latrines, sewerage, septic
tanks and shallow sewers) and options for site layout. The options
are costed and recommendations on selection made.

INFRASTRUCTURE/ECONOMICS/SRI LANKA

1430

FACILITATING THE PROVISION OF SERVICES IN URBAN
AREAS

WRAY A.   1989

Unpublished preprint in
EMERGING TRENDS IN THIRD WORLD HOUSING
POLICIES
CDPS
UNIVERSITY OF SHEFFIELD
6TH INTER SCHOOLS CONFERENCE ON DEVELOPMENT
18-19 MARCH 1989

Standards and technologies used in the provision of infrastructure
which facilitate institutional support and community participation
are described.

SERVICES/INSTITUTIONS/COMMUNITY PARTICIPATION/
COSTA RICA/GUATEMALA

1431

THE PROVISION OF BASIC MUNICIPAL
INFRASTRUCTURE THROUGH THE FOOD FOR WORK
PROGRAMME (APT) GUATEMALA CITY   GUATEMALA

WRAY A.   1988 pp31

Unpublished report for
UNDP/UNCHS
UNITED NATIONS CENTRE FOR HUMAN SETTLEMENTS
NAIROBI

A report on a mission to Guatemala City with the aim of reviewing
projects in the marginal areas of the City. Details are given of
modifications of the project with a view to other municipal
programmes. The project components include - water, sewerage,
storm water drainage, roads and solid wastes. Details of project
implementation and recommendations including reduction of
infrastructure costs, and need for operation and maintenance are
also given.

WATER SUPPLY/SEWERS/DRAINAGE/SOLID WASTE/
ROADS/IMPLEMENTATION/COSTS/OPERATION/
MAINTENANCE/GUATEMALA

Section 2. GROUND PREPARATION

2101

DREDGING : A HANDBOOK FOR ENGINEERS

BRAY R.N. 1979 pp276

EDWARD ARNOLD
LONDON

This handbook includes sections on reclamation, soil types and
conditions of the fill, characteristics of the fill, containment,
placing, consolidation and compaction of the fill as well as
dredging methods.

HYDRAULIC FILL

2102

SELECTION DEVELOPMENT AND STABILISATION OF
SITES FOR BUILDINGS IN HILLSIDES

GUPTA V.P.   1986

JOURNAL OF THE INSTITUTE OF ENGINEERS VOL 66
(C15) p184-189
THE INSTITUTION OF ENGINEERS INDIA

The paper gives a list of points for deciding comparative suitability
of various sites including an assessment of possible problems and
preventative measures to maintain stability. Remedial measures
used on selected sites are described including stepped terrace
development.

SLOPING SITES/INDIA

2103

BUILDING ON SLOPES

HODGKINSON A.   1981

ARCHITECTS JOURNAL VOL 173 NO 14   p663-668
LONDON

Two types of land slide - circular, and mud flow are defined and
details are given of techniques for retaining of slopes using
retaining walls and foundations.

SLOPING SITES

2104

BUILDING ON MARGINAL AND DERELICT LAND

INSTITUTE OF CIVIL ENGINEERS CONFERENCE
GLASGOW MAY 1986 pp861

THOMAS TELFORD
LONDON

Technical notes are provided for building on hydraulic fills,
landfill sites, derelict sites of former industry and soft and loose
natural soils.

HYDRAULIC FILL/DERELICT LAND

2105

CONSTRUCTION OF AND ON COMPACTED FILLS

MONAHAN E. J.   1986

JOHN WILEY pp200
NEW YORK

This text book includes general sections on soil compaction, soil
testing and building codes. Specific attention is given to fill and
fill compaction including strength and stability, and problems
encountered with earth structures. Methods of controlling the fill
process and specifications are included.

GROUND FILL/CONSTRUCTION

2106

HOUSING ON SLOPING SITES: A DESIGN GUIDE

SIMPSON B.J.
PURDY M.T.   1984 pp190

CONSTRUCTION PRESS
LONDON

The introduction includes current practice and physical constraints
and opportunities to building on sloping land. Topics covered
include site planning for housing including roads and other
services and earthworks stability on slopes.

SLOPING SITES/UK

SEE 1104
SEE 1107
SEE 1108
SEE 1110

Ground Preparation

2201

GROUND SLOPE COST CURVES

GEE K.

CHARTERED MUNICIPAL ENGINEER. VOL.89 1962
p299-301 appendix p 302-340
INSTITUTION OF MUNICIPAL ENGINEERS LONDON

The effects of slope on the cost of houses and roads is explored
and tabulated for each of the components including roads, house
excavation, concrete, brickwork and the sub-structure.

SLOPING SITES/COSTS/UK

SEE 1410
SEE 1429

Section 3. DRAINAGE

3101

URBAN SULLAGE IN DEVELOPING COUNTRIES

ASHWORTH J.   1982

WATERLINES VOL 1 NO 2 p14-16
INTERMEDIATE TECHNOLOGY PUBLICATIONS
LONDON

The article describes the nature of sullage and existing methods of disposal with the resulting consequences of uncontrolled disposal. After a description of water transmitted diseases, appropriate methods of disposal are described, using small bore sewers and improved washing slabs. Cost recovery, education and administration are also considered.

SULLAGE/SULLAGE DISPOSAL/SMALL BORE SEWERS/
WASHING SLABS

3102

DRAINAGE OF ASPHALTIC PAVEMENT STRUCTURES

MANUAL SERIES No 15 (MS-15) 1984 pp118

THE ASPHALT INSTITUTE
MARYLAND, USA

After an introduction defining the types of drainage, surface and sub-surface drainage are described with sections on design, maintenance and U.S. practice.

DRAINAGE/ASPHALT

3103

SURFACE IRRIGATION: OPEN DISTRIBUTION SYSTEMS

BOOHER L.J. 1974 CHAPTER 4 p31-52

FOOD AND AGRICULTURE ORGANISATION

The design of both lined and unlined open channel distribution systems together with their associated structures is detailed.

DRAINAGE/STORMWATER OPTIONS/CHANNELS/
CHANNEL LINING

3104

DESIGN OF REINFORCED GRASS WATERWAYS

BORMAN L.A.
BRAMLEY M.E.
HEWLETT H.W.M. 1987   pp116

CIRI/A REPORT 116
CONSTRUCTION INDUSTRY RESEARCH AND
INFORMATION
LONDON

Methods of reinforcing grass lined waterways using either geotextiles or cellular concrete are described in order to reduce erosion by high velocity flow. Hydraulic, geotechnical and botanical aspects are considered and worked examples illustrating design procedures are given. Data from full-scale trials on prototype reinforced grass channels are provided.

DRAINAGE/CHANNELS/GEOTEXTILES/

3105

BUILDING DRAINAGE

BS 8301 1985 pp61

BRITISH STANDARDS INSTITUTION

The standard definitions of materials and components and design and installation recommendations for foul, surface, combined and groundwater drainage. Guidance on site installation, maintenance and testing are also given.

DRAINAGE/BUILDINGS

3106

MAIN DRAINAGE SYSTEMS

DORT van J.A.
BOS M.G.

LAND DRAINAGE CONFERENCE VOL.4 1974 pp123
INTERNATIONAL INSTITUTE FOR LAND RECLAMATION
AND IMPROVEMENT
WAGENINGEN, NETHERLANDS

This paper considers the design of a main land drainage system. Sections include - stability of drainage canals, velocities, shapes and protection against scour, flow velocity control, flow control structures.

DRAINAGE/CHANNELS

3107

THE ADAPTATION OF THE RRL HYDROGRAPH METHOD
FOR TROPICAL CONDITIONS

FORD W.G.   1975 p409-457

TRANSPORT AND ROAD RESEARCH LABORATORY
REPORT SR 259
DEPARTMENT OF ENVIRONMENT
LONDON

The RRL Hydrograph method provides an accurate method for
runoff predictions from paved areas. Modifications to the method
based on data obtained from instrumented catchments in Nairobi,
Kenya and Kampala, Uganda are described which allow for the
contribution of unpaved areas which are of significance in many
tropical countries.

RAINFALL/RUN-OFF

3108

DRAINAGE OF SLOPING LAND

HOORN van J.W.
MOLEN van der W.H.

LAND DRAINAGE CONFERENCE VOL.4 1974 p326-329
INTERNATIONAL INSTITUTE FOR LAND RECLAMATION
AND IMPROVEMENT
WAGENINGEN, NETHERLANDS

The principles of drainage of sloping land are discussed together
with the design of appropriate interception drainage.

DRAINAGE/SLOPING SITES

3109

GREYWATER TREATMENT

KABBASH A.   1977   pp29

RENEWABLE RESOURCES PROJECT
MCGILL UNIVERSITY
MONTREAL

The design of a greywater filter system is described and tested.
There is a note on possible methods of discarding the greywater or
of reusing it.

SULLAGE DISPOSAL/REUSE

3110

MANUAL OF SURFACE DRAINAGE ENGINEERING

KINORI B.Z. 1970 pp209

ELSEVIER PUBLICATIONS

This book includes sections on the hydraulics of open channels,
scour, slope of channel walls, stable earth channels, and different
channel lining options including vegetation, compacted or cement
stabilised soil, masonry, concrete and asphaltic materials.

DRAINAGE/STORMWATER OPTIONS/CHANNELS/
CHANNEL LINING

3111

IRRIGATION ENGINEERING: CANALS AND BARRAGES

LELIAVSKY S. 1965 pp297

CHAPMAN AND HALL

The technical design of canals and drains including flow control
structures is detailed with consideration of alignment, water
levels, surface areas, and longitudinal design. Although aimed at
irrigation it contains information of value for urban drainage.

DRAINAGE/CHANNELS

3112

STORMWATER DRAINAGE FOR LOW-INCOME GROUP
TOWNSHIPS

MILES L. C.   1984 p29-39

MUNICIPAL ENGINEER VOL 15 (4)

Stormwater drainage in low-income communities maximises the
use of non-structural measures such as using the natural properties
of the terrain to reduce costs. The drainage system may serve
several functions and has a profound influence on road layout.

DRAINAGE/STORMWATER OPTIONS

3113

DESIGN OF STREET CHANNELS

NEBIKER J.H.
AZIMI H.A.

TECHNICAL REPORT No 53-001 1974 pp28
PAHLAVI UNIVERSITY
DEPARTMENT OF CIVIL ENGINEERING SHIRAZ, IRAN

Multi-purpose lined street channels in Iran for stormwater, shade
and tree irrigation are described. The report includes sections on
design flows, hydraulic design, critical flow, special head loss. and
construction.

DRAINAGE/CHANNELS/STORMWATER OPTIONS/IRAN

3114

LINING OF EARTHEN IRRIGATION CHANNELS

SALLY H.L. 1965 pp109

ASIA PUBLISHING HOUSE
LONDON

Along with the advantages of different lined channels procedures
for their design and construction using different materials are
described under Indian practice.

DRAINAGE/LINING/CHANNEL LINING

3115

DRAINAGE OF AGRICULTURAL LAND: CHAPTER 3
SURFACE DRAINAGE

SOIL CONSERVATION SERVICE
UNITED STATES DEPARTMENT OF AGRICULTURE 1973
pp99-120

Surface drainage systems and layouts are described with
definitions of the different types of ditch and their function.
Guidance is also given on the design, construction and
maintenance of open drainage channels.

DRAINAGE/CHANNELS

3116

TRANSPORT AND ROAD RESEARCH LABORATORY,
ROAD NOTE 35
A GUIDE FOR ENGINEERS TO THE DESIGN OF STORM
SEWER SYSTEMS

TRRL 1976 pp30

TRANSPORT AND ROAD RESEARCH LABORATORY
BERKSHIRE

The rational (Lloyd Davis) method and the T.R.R.L. Hydrograph
method for the design of storm sewers are detailed.

DRAINAGE/STORM SEWERS

3117

MANUAL OF GREYWATER TREATMENT PRACTICE

WINNEBERGER J.H.T   1974   pp102

ANN ARBOR SCIENCE
MICHIGAN

Part I describes on site treatment, subsurface disposal including
disposal field systems on flat and sloping ground, disposal pits and

percolation tests. There are appendices on soil absorption and a
guide to estimating soil potential.

Part II investigates the separation of water borne wastes, the
characteristics and pollution aspects of household greywater and
soil mantle purification.

SULLAGE/SULLAGE DISPOSAL/SULLAGE TREATMENT/
PERCOLATION

3118

SURFACE WATER DRAINAGE FOR LOW INCOME
COMMUNITIES

WORLD HEALTH ORGANISATION
UNEP

WHO, GENEVA, 1991.
A detailed examination of surface water drainage for low-income
communities particularly as it relates to health and environmental
hygiene.

COMMUNITY PARTICIPATION/URBAN AREAS/MAINTENANCE

SEE 1102
SEE 1103
SEE 1105
SEE 1107
SEE 1108
SEE 1109
SEE 1110
SEE 1111
SEE 1112
SEE 1113
SEE 4120
SEE 5107
SEE 5113
SEE 6107
SEE 6124
SEE 6128

3201

THE NATURE OF SULLAGE

FEACHEM R.G.
BRADLEY D.J.
GARELICK H.
MARA D.D. 1980 p27-29

HEALTH ASPECTS OF EXCRETA AND SULLAGE
MANAGEMENT
WORLD BANK
WASHINGTON DC

The section includes details of the quantities of sullage generated,
the characteristics of sullage and the health aspects including
disposal on site and through a drainage system.

SULLAGE DISPOSAL/HEALTH

3202

URBAN DRAINAGE STRATEGIES FOR SMALL
COMMUNITIES IN DEVELOPING COUNTRIES

GROTTKER, MATTHIAS
KHELIL, AMAR

NAT. SCI. TECH. VOL 22 NO 3/4, p283-290, 1990

INSTITUTE FUR WASSERWIRTSCHAFT, HYDROLOGIE
AND LANDWIRTCHAFTLICHEN; UNIVERSITAT
HANNOVER

The paper points out the interactions of small waste water
treatment plants within an urban drainage system, stressing the
different characteristics of catchment areas in developing and
industrialised countries.

DRAINAGE

3203

DRAINAGE OPTIONS FOR NEIGHBOURHOODS

NIMPUNO K.   1982

INSTITUTE FOR HOUSING STUDIES
ROTTERDAM

This mimeo is quoted in the UNCHS publication Community
Participation and Low-cost Drainage, see 3204.

DRAINAGE

3204

COMMUNITY PARTICIPATION AND LOW COST
DRAINAGE

UNCHS TRAINING MODULE 1986 pp59
HS/97/86/E

UNITED NATIONS CENTRE FOR HUMAN SETTLEMENTS
NAIROBI

Low cost drainage systems including options, designs, steep
slopes and flat land are described. Included are sections on drain
design, and community participation in planning, construction and
systems maintenance.

DRAINAGE/SLOPING SITES/COMMUNITY PARTICIPATION

SEE 1204
SEE 1230
SEE 1236

SEE 6208
SEE 6205

3301

CONSTRUCTION AND MAINTENANCE OF SIMPLE
DRAINAGE SYSTEMS

SCHILDERMAN T. 1980

DAR ES SALAAM CENTRE FOR HOUSING STUDIES
ARDHI INSTITUTE
DAR ES SALAAM

This mimeo is quoted in the UNCHS publication Community
Participation and Low-cost Drainage, see 3204.

DRAINAGE

3302

APPLICATION OF FERROCEMENT DRAINAGE FLUME IN
SLUM UPGRADING

MANOHARN S.   1982 p373-383

JOURNAL OF FERROCEMENT VOL12 NO4
ASIAN INSTITUTE OF TECHNOLOGY
BANGKOK

The report describes two types of prefabricated drainage flume
developed by the National Housing Authority of Thailand.

DRAINAGE/CHANNELS/FERROCEMENT/COSTS

3303

HEALTH HAZARDS AND POLLUTION FROM OPEN
DRAINS IN A NIGERIAN CITY

SRIDHAR M.K.C
OLUWANDE P.A.
OKUBADEJO A.O.   1981   p29-33

AMBIO VOL 10 NO 1
STOCKHOLM

An account is given of the chemical and microbiological
characteristics of wastewater flowing in open drains in Ibadan,
Nigeria. Faecal coliform counts were as high as 18,000 per 100ml
and both protozoan and helminthic parasites were detected; in
addition to the health hazard, pollution of surface and groundwater
is probable.

DRAINAGE/SULLAGE/HEALTH/NIGERIA

SEE 4302

3401

HIGHWAY ENGINEERING TECHNICAL REPORT ANNEX 2:
TENTATIVE GUIDELINES FOR THE DRAINAGE OF ROADS
BINLIOG VOL 3 84-3748

CHANDRASEKHARAN E.C. 1982 pp11

Unpublished report
UNCHS and UNDP
UNITED NATIONS CENTRE FOR HUMAN SETTLEMENTS
NAIROBI

An annex to a technical report which details drainage of roads in
the United Arab Emirates. Data is given on drain design and
discussion of the need and appropriateness of surface, sub-surface
and cross drainage systems.

DRAINAGE/ROADS/UNITED ARAB EMIRATES

3402

DRAINAGE PROBLEMS OF A PACIFIC ISLAND

EVANS J.G.

COLLABORATION IN WATER AND WASTE FOR
DEVELOPING COUNTRIES
5th WEDC CONFERENCE LOUGHBOROUGH 1979 p89-105
LOUGHBOROUGH UNIVERSITY OF TECHNOLOGY

This report describes the problem of wastewater disposal in
Nuku'alofa, Samoa. Issues discussed include wastewater disposal
from hotels and hospitals, ground levels, surface water drainage,
sewers and wastewater treatment facilities including septic tank
sludge treatment.

DRAINAGE/SULLAGE/EFFLUENT

3403

IMPROVEMENT OF JAKARA VALLEY DRAINAGE,
NIGERIA

HASSAN A. 1985

Unpublished MSc thesis pp109
LOUGHBOROUGH UNIVERSITY OF TECHNOLOGY

A review of the drainage problems in Jakara valley with possible
solutions. Topics covered include background information,
existing drainage facilities, criteria for drainage design, flood
prevention and channel lining.

DRAINAGE/CHANNELS/CHANNEL LINING/NIGERIA

3404

RECOMMENDATIONS FOR THE IMPROVEMENT OF ROAD
DRAINAGE AND ROAD PAVEMENTS FOR MALE
(MALDIVES)
UNCHS BIBLIOG 1984 VOL3 84-4182

SECKINGTON C.C.   1983 pp90

GRABOWSKY & POORT
THE HAGUE
NETHERLANDS

This report discusses road construction and maintenance in relation
to drainage in an area of high rainfall. Pipe systems and soakaways
are reviewed and recommendations made regarding road building
materials and the location of drainage and under road utilities.

DRAINAGE/ROADS/PIPES/SOAKAWAYS/MALDIVES

SEE 1403
SEE 1406
SEE 1407
SEE 1408
SEE 1410
SEE 1409
SEE 1414
SEE 1417
SEE 1412
SEE 1420
SEE 1421
SEE 1422
SEE 1424
SEE 1426
SEE 1427
SEE 6431
SEE 6428

Section 4. ROADS AND ACCESS

4101

ROADWORK TECHNOLOGY VOL1

ARNISON J.H. 1967   pp148

ILIFFE BOOKS
LONDON

The history and development of road construction is described.
Topics covered include kerbs and kerbing materials (including
stone and precast concrete), setting out and layout, block paving
including bases and laying, footpaths (including stone and precast
concrete) and plant and equipment required.

ROAD CONSTRUCTION/STONE PAVING/
CONCRETE PAVING

4102

RESIDENTIAL ACCESS DESIGN

BROWN A.M.

MUNICIPAL ENGINEER VOL 5 (2) 1988 p61-76
LONDON

The article summarises residential access design in the United
Kingdom. Consideration is given to design criteria, the problems
of the interaction of traffic and pedestrians and the design process.

ACCESS

4103

CONCRETE PAVEMENTS FOR LOW TRAFFIC VOLUMES

CARTER K.E.   1967

CIVIL ENGINEERING VOL 37 NO 2 p58-59
AMERICAN SOCIETY OF CIVIL ENGINEERS
NEW YORK

The use of 150mm thick unreinforced concrete pavements is
described in rural Iowa. After experiments with 100mm, 125mm
and 137mm thicknesses, the 150mm was found to be suitable for
carrying 125 to 600 vehicles per day with limited numbers of
single axle loads up to 7,300kg.

CONCRETE PAVING

4104

HOUSING ESTATE ROADS

CEMENT & CONCRETE ASSOCIATION 1961 pp33

CEMENT AND CONCRETE ASSOCIATION
SLOUGH

This report includes sections on the method of construction,
earthwork preparation, bases, slab design, services and gullies
and maintenance considerations.

ROAD CONSTRUCTION/MAINTENANCE/
CONCRETE PAVING

4105

ROADS IN URBAN AREAS

DEPARTMENT OF ENVIRONMENT 1983 pp96

HMSO DOE 736323 C15 3/83
LONDON

This report considers the engineering requirements of urban
traffic and the urban road system under the following headings
of classification, alignment, cross-sections   for various
distribution and access roads, road equipment, and the location
and jointing of sewers and public utilities.

ACCESS/SEWERS/PUBLIC UTILITIES/
SERVICE LOCATION/LAYOUT

4106

RESIDENTIAL ROADS & FOOTPATHS
LAYOUT CONSIDERATIONS

DEPARTMENT OF ENVIRONMENT/DEPARTMENT OF
TRANSPORT DESIGN BULLETIN 32   1977 pp75

HMSO DOE 0598249 K402/80
LONDON

Important issues discussed in the report include relating the
scheme to its setting (including vehicle movement and site
characteristics), minimising danger and nuisance from non access
traffic, reducing speed and making provision for pedestrians, and
off street parking. Consideration also needs to be given to
providing for vehicle movement including   carriageway widths
and statutory and other services.

ACCESS/PARKING/SERVICES/CIRCULATION

4107

CONCRETE ROADS

4107

CONCRETE ROADS
DESIGN AND CONSTRUCTION

DEPT OF SCIENTIFIC AND INDUSTRIAL RESEARCH
ROAD RESEARCH LABORATORY 1955   pp404

HMSO
LONDON

The design of the structure, and joints and construction of concrete
roads are described in some detail with sections on the properties
and testing of concrete, cements and aggregates. Other issues
covered include mix design, and quality control, as influences on
durability. Slab stresses, defects and maintenance are also
considered as well as the requirements for construction equipment.

ROAD DESIGN/ROAD CONSTRUCTION/CONCRETE PAVING
/MAINTENANCE

4108

EXTERNAL PAVING

DUELL J.   1981   p861-869

ARCHITECTS JOURNAL VOL 173 NO 18
LONDON

Details of various types of paving are given together with an
assessment of their performance on the basis of cost.

ROAD CONSTRUCTION/BLOCK PAVING/COSTS

4109

STABILISED EARTH ROADS

KEZDI A. 1979 pp327

ELSEVIER SCIENTIFIC PUBLICATIONS
OXFORD

This book begins by describing the importance of stabilised
roads, with reference to their historical background and
commonly used methods. Physical and chemical aspects are
discussed in sections under testing, mechanical and chemical
stabilisation (cement, lime, bitumen). Guidance on the design of
stabilised earth roads includes pavement design and strength,
with recommendations on construction procedures for mixing,
compaction and control.

ROAD CONSTRUCTION/STABILISED EARTH

4110

PAVING THE WAY

KNAPTON J.   1981   p419-421

ARCHITECTS JOURNAL VOL 174 NO 34
LONDON

This article provides an overview of paving with consideration of
the history of paving, the advantages of brick paving, selection of
sub-base material, recommended paving practice and the
requirement for maintenance.

ROAD CONSTRUCTION/BLOCK PAVING/MAINTENANCE

4111

CONCRETE BLOCK PAVING FOR LIGHTLY TRAFFICKED
ROADS AND PAVED AREAS

LILLEY A.A.
CLARK A.J. 1980 pp16

BRITISH CEMENT ASSOCIATION
SLOUGH

Both structural and detailed design (including specification of the
strength and dimension of block) are described together with such
construction issues as sub-base preparation, laying, and
reinstatement of blocks.

ROAD CONSTRUCTION/CONCRETE PAVING

4112

SURFACING FOR LOW VOLUME ROADS IN DEVELOPING
COUNTRIES

MILLARD R.S.   1982

WORLD HIGHWAYS VOL XXIII NO 1 p4-6
INTERNATIONAL ROAD FEDERATION

The paper explores the criteria currently used to decide whether
low-volume roads are to be provided with asphalt or concrete road
surfaces, and examines some of the materials and techniques used
for these roads in the context of west Africa.

ROAD CONSTRUCTION

4113

LOW COST ROADS

ODIER L
MILLARD R.S.
MEHRA S.R.
SANTOS P.D. 1971 pp158

BUTTERWORTHS
LONDON

This text includes sections on road planning, geometric design, materials and pavement design (including stabilised roads and drainage), permanent surfaces (gravel and stone bases, stabilised soils, bituminous surfacings, concrete roads), pavement design, road drainage and maintenance.

ROAD DESIGN/ROAD CONSTRUCTION/
STABILISED EARTH/GRAVEL ROADS/BITUMEN ROADS
/CONCRETE PAVING/MAINTENANCE/DRAINAGE

4114

HIGHWAY ENGINEERING

OGLESBY C.H.
HICKS R.G.   1982   pp844

JOHN WILEY
NEW YORK

This comprehensive text includes sections on drainage (covering road drainage in urban areas, channels, dikes and culverts), construction of the road bed (including fill, marshy ground and construction in developing countries), and selection of aggregate and surface materials covering gravel and crushed rock, stabilised roads, base courses, macadam surfaces, and bituminous and concrete pavements.

ROAD DESIGN/ROAD CONSTRUCTION/GRAVEL/
STABILISED EARTH/BITUMEN ROADS/
CONCRETE PAVING/DRAINAGE

4116

ROAD MAKING MATERIALS AND PAVEMENT DESIGN IN TROPICAL AND SUB TROPICAL COUNTRIES

O'REILLY M.P.
MILLARD R.S.

TRRL REPORT LR 279   1969
TRANSPORT AND ROAD RESEARCH LABORATORY
BERKSHIRE

Design, material selection and maintenance issues are discussed for both unimproved and improved roads with permanent or temporary surfaces. Topics covered include requirements for mechanical stabilisation and drainage, base and sub-bases for flexible roads including gravel, stone and stabilised soil and procedures for bituminous surfacing including priming and dressing. Concrete roads are also outlined as is pavement design including drainage for flexible roads.

PAVEMENT DESIGN/ROAD CONSTRUCTION/
GRAVEL ROADS/STONE PAVING/STABILISED EARTH/
BITUMEN ROADS/CONCRETE PAVING/DRAINAGE

4117

CONCRETE PAVEMENTS

STOCK A.F. (ed.) 1988 pp433

ELSEVIER APPLIED SCIENCE
LONDON

Chapter 11 includes a discussion of the nature of block paving and its advantages and characteristics. Guidelines are given for pavement design, construction, and maintenance in a range of situations including a residential street. Their performance under traffic loadings is detailed.

ROAD CONSTRUCTION/BLOCK PAVING/MAINTENANCE

4118

A GUIDE TO THE STRUCTURAL DESIGN OF PAVEMENTS FOR NEW ROADS

ROAD NOTE 29   1970   pp36

TRANSPORT AND ROAD RESEARCH LABORATORY
BERKSHIRE

The selection and design of pavement types, including flexible, concrete and concrete with a bituminous surface, is detailed.

ROAD DESIGN/PAVING/CONCRETE PAVING/
BITUMEN ROADS

4119

A GUIDE TO THE STRUCTURAL DESIGN OF BITUMEN SURFACED ROADS IN TROPICAL & SUB TROPICAL COUNTRIES

ROAD NOTE 31 1977 pp26

TRANSPORT AND ROAD RESEARCH LABORATORY
BERKSHIRE

The design and specification of flexible paving is detailed with topics covered including design estimation of the number and axle loads of vehicles, establishing the required subgrade and pavement strength and the requirement for drainage. Alternative base materials including natural gravels, crusted stone, and stabilised soils, and surfacings including dressings and premixed bituminous materials are also described.

ROAD DESIGN/STABILISED EARTH/GRAVEL ROADS/
STONE PAVING/BITUMEN ROADS

4120

GUIDELINES ON DESIGN OF CIRCULATION IN LOW
INCOME URBAN SETTLEMENTS

UNCHS HS/88/85/E 1985 pp45

UNITED NATIONS CENTRE FOR HUMAN SETTLEMENTS
NAIROBI

The typical urban road system is classified together with layouts,
road cross sections and alignments. The provision of parking and
pedestrian facilities is outlined together with pavement design
principals (structure and materials), surface water drainage (drain
design and construction. Tables and drawings are used to describe
typical pavement structures in selected low-income urban projects
and road cross sections and siting of services.

ACCESS/CIRCULATION/ROAD DESIGN/DRAINAGE

SEE 1103
SEE 1104
SEE 1107
SEE 1108
SEE 1109
SEE 1110
SEE 1111
SEE 1112
SEE 1113

4201

ECONOMIC DESIGN OF LOW TRAFFIC ROADS

OECD 1986 pp128

ORGANISATION FOR ECONOMIC COOPERATION AND
DEVELOPMENT
PARIS

A review of research and practice on geometric design standards
for roads with traffic volumes less than 1500 vehicles per day,
extending to an overall design methodology for low-traffic roads.
Future research needs and the case for the developing countries
discussed.

ROAD DESIGN/STANDARDS

4202

UNDERSTANDING SLUMS

RYBCZYNSKI W.
BHATT V.

OPEN HOUSE INTERNATIONAL VOL.11 [1] 1986. p6-16.
SCHOOL OF ARCHITECTURE
UNIVERSITY OF NEWCASTLE UPON TYNE

A study of space in relation to the expansion of dwellings and
workshops, public spaces and vehicle access. A rationale for
street classification and vehicle/pedestrian access is described
supported with tabulated data including figures on vehicle
dimensions.

ROAD DESIGN/ACCESS/VEHICLES

SEE 1204
SEE 1106

4301

HIGHWAY CONSTRUCTION DETAILS

DEPARTMENT OF TRANSPORT
SCOTTISH DEVELOPMENT DEPT
WELSH OFFICE
DEPARTMENT OF THE ENVIRONMENT FOR NORTHERN
IRELAND   1987

HMSO   pp161
LONDON

This report presents standard drawings and details for trunk roads
and highways. Included are typical highway cross-sections,
pavement details, details on concrete and flexible (bitumen)
carriage-ways, the provision of drainage and underground cable
ducts.

ROAD CONSTRUCTION/PAVING/DRAINAGE

4302

EARTH ROADS - THEIR CONSTRUCTION AND
MAINTENANCE

HINDSON J. 1983   pp123

INTERMEDIATE TECHNOLOGY PUBLICATIONS
LONDON

The location of earth roads, their construction and maintenance
(including rehabilitation) are detailed along with the need for
erosion prevention, soil conservation and the provision of
drainage. Both village and market roads are discussed and specific
drainage and water control methods considered include diversion
banks, lead off drains and drifts.

ROAD CONSTRUCTION/EARTH ROADS/DRAINAGE/
MAINTENANCE

4303

GRAVEL ROADS - TECHNIQUES OF CONSTRUCTION

MINISTRY OF HIGHWAYS, SRI LANKA 1986   pp10

GOVERNMENT PRESS
COLOMBO
SRI LANKA

A simple guide to use of gravel roads in Sri Lanka, primarily in rural areas but of value for unpaved cluster roads in urban communities.

ROAD CONSTRUCTION/GRAVEL ROADS/MAINTENANCE

4304

MAINTENANCE MANAGEMENT FOR DISTRICT
ENGINEERS

TRRL   1987   pp62
OVERSEAS ROAD NOTE 1

TRANSPORT AND ROAD RESEARCH LABORATORY
BERKSHIRE

The role of the engineer in maintenance and management activities is discussed. Topics covered include maintenance of inventory, inspection procedures, determination of road maintenance schedules, defining available resources, identification of priorities as well as work scheduling and monitoring.

ROAD MAINTENANCE

4305

MAINTENANCE TECHNIQUES FOR ROAD ENGINEERS

TRRL   1985   pp42
OVERSEAS ROAD NOTE 2

TRANSPORT AND ROAD RESEARCH LABORATORY
BERKSHIRE

Maintenance methods are detailed in relation to the maintenance of road furniture, drainage structures, shoulders, slopes, unpaved roads and paved roads.

ROAD MAINTENANCE/DRAINAGE/SLOPING SITES

4306

A GUIDE TO SURFACE DRESSING IN TROPICAL AND SUB
- TROPICAL COUNTRIES

TRRL   1982   pp33
OVERSEAS ROAD NOTE 3

TRANSPORT AND ROAD RESEARCH LABORATORY
BERKSHIRE

General design principles of surface dressing are described including material selection, establishing chip size and rate of spread, plant and equipment requirements, typical dressing processes along with alternative surface treatments.

ROAD CONSTRUCTION

4307

A GUIDE TO ROAD PROJECT APPRAISAL

TRRL   1988   pp97
OVERSEAS ROAD NOTE 5

TRANSPORT AND ROAD RESEARCH LABORATORY
BERKSHIRE

A comprehensive planning manual intended for administrators, economists, transport planners and engineers. The note deals primarily with rural road projects from new construction through upgrading, rehabilitation, stage construction and maintenance. Some technical design information is applicable to urban communities.

ROAD DESIGN

4308

A GUIDE TO CONCRETE ROAD CONSTRUCTION

TRANSPORT AND ROAD RESEARCH LABORATORY
(DEPT OF TRANSPORT)
CEMENT & CONCRETE ASSOCIATION 3RD EDITION 1978
pp82

HMSO
LONDON

The areas covered in detail include road design, including base and slab thickness and layout, the selection and properties of sub bases and grades, details on reinforcement, joints and the control of concrete quality.

ROAD CONSTRUCTION/CONCRETE PAVING

4401

URBAN OPEN SPACES PROJECT   DODOMA

UNCHS BIBLIOG 4 1986 86-4295 REPORTS 1-10

LEMAN GROUP INC   1984
TORONTO

Design guidelines for the development of pedestrian walkways

are presented particularly in relation   to   the   requirement for
stormwater drainage. Recommendations on design are included.

ACCESS/PEDESTRIANS/DRAINAGE/TANZANIA

SEE 1407
SEE 1406
SEE 1410
SEE 1414
SEE 1417
SEE 1412
SEE 1420
SEE 1421
SEE 1422
SEE 1424
SEE 1427

Section 5. WATER SUPPLY

5101

COMMUNITY WATER SUPPLY
THE HANDPUMP OPTION

ARLOSOROFF S.
TSCHANNEREL G.
GREY D.
JOURNEY W.
KARP A.
LANGENEFFER O.
ROCHE R.   1987 pp202.

WORLD BANK
WASHINGTON DC

This document will assist with the choice of handpump technology
(of limited value in urban areas) during the project planning and
implementation phases. It is based on a review of community
water supply options and the performance of existing handpump
technology. A worked example of the selection of a handpump
given technical and institutional constraints is presented.

ABSTRACTION OPTIONS/HANDPUMPS

5102

HAND DRILLED WELLS
A MANUAL ON SITING,DESIGN,CONSTRUCTION AND
MAINTENANCE

BLANKWAARDT B.   1984   pp132

RWEGARULILA WATER RESOURCES INSTITUTE
DAR ES SALAAM

This manual provides comprehensive treatment of hand well
drilling techniques beginning with a description of hand dug
versus drilled wells. Sections are included on groundwater, drilling
in unconsolidated sediments, site investigation techniques,
suggested criteria for borehole approval and the design of
tubewells including their components and design principles.
Drilling operations are also described together with the installation
of the system, necessary testing and backfilling, construction of the
ground slab and the installation and maintenance of the handpump.

WELLS/HANDPUMPS/MAINTENANCE

5103

SQUATTER AREA UPGRADING IN MALAYSIA

BRADLEY R.M.
PONNIAH C.D.   1988

WATER AND URBAN SERVICES IN ASIA AND THE
PACIFIC
14th WEDC CONFERENCE   KUALA LUMPUR   p107-110
LOUGHBOROUGH UNIVERSITY OF TECHNOLOGY

Issues discussed include the socio-economic status of the
inhabitants and different upgrading strategies including the rate of
implementation along with financial aspects. Water and sanitation
options are detailed including standpipes, pour flush, pit and
communal latrines, sullage disposal and night soil systems.

STANDPOSTS/POUR FLUSH LATRINES/
COMMUNAL LATRINES/SULLAGE/FINANCE/MALAYSIA

5104

ENVIRONMENTAL HEALTH ENGINEERING IN THE
TROPICS

CAIRNCROSS A.M.
FEACHEM R.G.   1983   pp283

JOHN WILEY
CHICHESTER

An introductory text covering a wide range of topics with
particular value for low-income communities. Urban water
distribution and water demand management is considered
including tariff policy. Excreta disposal systems and programmes
for latrine construction are detailed.

WATER SUPPLY/SANITATION/SOLID WASTE/HEALTH

5105

SMALL WATER SUPPLIES

CAIRNCROSS A.M.
FEACHEM R.G.   1978 pp 78

ROSS INSTITUTE BULLETIN 10
LONDON

Covering the whole range of small water supplies, areas of interest
to low-income urban communities include sections on water
storage, pipes and pipe laying, water distribution, house
connections and public standposts. Purification of water within the
home is also considered.

WATER DISTRIBUTION/PURIFICATION/WATER STORAGE

5106

LOW COST DISTRIBUTION SYSTEMS

de AZEVEDO NETTO J.M.   p257-272

IN: IRC BULLETIN 10
INTERNATIONAL TRAINING SEMINAR ON COMMUNTITY

INTERNATIONAL TRAINING SEMINAR ON COMMUNTITY
WATER SUPPLY IN DEVELOPING COUNTRIES
WHO INTERNATIONAL REFERENCE CENTRE FOR
COMMUNITY WATER SUPPLY AND SANITATION, 1977
THE HAGUE

Given particular patterns of water consumption and resulting
fluctuations in flow recommendations are made of minimum sizes
of water mains. A worked example is provided and economic
models of distribution networks presented.

WATER MAINS/WATER DISTRIBUTION

5107

WATER AND SANITATION IN SLUMS AND SHANTY
TOWNS

ETHERTON D.   1980

UNICEF REPORT TRH 10 pp98
UNITED NATIONS CHILDREN'S FUND
NEW YORK

Existing water and sanitation conditions are described together
with the opportunities for planning improvements including the
likely costs of any new technology. Specific technology options in
water supply and distribution, sewerage, sullage and waste
treatment are detailed and their suitability discussed, including
water supply collection and treatment, excreta disposal (by bucket
latrines, vaults, pit latrines, pour flush, aqua privies, septic tanks,
stabilisation ponds and communal latrines), stormwater drainage
and solid waste disposal.

SULLAGE/STORMWATER OPTIONS/SANITATION OPTIONS
STABILISATION PONDS/SOLID WASTE/COSTS/
WATER SUPPLY

5108

WATER AND WASTEWATER TECHNOLOGY

HAMMER M.J.   1986   pp536

JOHN WILEY
CHICHESTER

Water distribution systems are discussed in terms of required
quantity and pressure including fire requirements. Sections are
included on well construction, pipe networks, design layouts, and
evaluation of distribution systems. The characteristics of
wastewater flow, and collection systems associated with it are also
covered together with system operation.

FIRE HYDRANTS/PIPES/OPERATION/SEWERS/WELLS/
SERVICE CONNECTIONS

5109

A DESIGN APPROACH TO REDUCE PIPELINE
REQUIREMENT IN WATER DISTRIBUTION SYSTEMS

HUSTON M.J.

AFRICAN WATER AND SEWAGE VOL 2 [1] 1983 p30-34

FUEL AND METALLURGICAL JOURNALS
SURREY

A cost saving design method is described which reduces the
diameter of the pipeline by increasing the balancing storage. This
is more applicable to rural areas where the lengths of pipework
involved comprise the greatest portion of the cost.

WATER DISTRIBUTION/PIPES/WATER STORAGE/KENYA

5110

WATER DISTRIBUTION SYSTEMS

WATER PRACTICE MANUAL NO 4   1984 pp450

INSTITUTION OF WATER ENGINEERS AND SCIENTISTS
LONDON

The manual describes design philosophy and principles, along with
bylaws and consumer requirements which determine the
performance requirements of water distribution systems.
Technical subjects covered include network analysis, pumping
plant selection, pipework and main laying together with
maintenance and leakage detection.

WATER DISTRIBUTION/PUMPING/NETWORK ANALYSIS/
MAINTENANCE

5111

WATER SUPPLY AND SANITATION IN DEVELOPING
COUNTRIES

WATER PRACTICE MANUAL NO 3   1983 pp413

INSTITUTION OF WATER ENGINEERS AND SCIENTISTS
LONDON

Maintenance, operation and administration of water and
wastewater systems are discussed in this publication with
emphasis on procedures and systems. Topics covered in some
detail include the keeping of records of permanent construction
and completed operation and   maintenance, operational staffing
requirements and necessary plant and equipment, workshops, and
purchasing and stores for an ongoing maintenance programme.

WATER SUPPLY/WASTE WATER DISPOSAL/OPERATION/
MAINTENANCE

5112

HANDPUMPS: ISSUES AND CONCEPTS IN RURAL WATER
SUPPLY PROGRAMMES

IRC TECHNICAL PAPER 25 1988 pp163

IRC, INTERNATIONAL REFERENCE CENTRE, THE
HAGUE/IDRC,INTERNATIONAL DEVELOPMENT
RESEARCH CENTRE CANADA

The current state of handpump technology is described with
details of the types of handpump in use. Particular emphasis is
given to issues such as the administration of rural water supply
programmes, including planning for sustainability, decision
making with the community, siting and construction of wells, and
handpump installation and maintenance. This approach has some
value for urban projects.

HANDPUMPS/COMMUNITY PARTICIPATION

5113

PUBLIC STANDPOST WATER SUPPLY
A DESIGN MANUAL

IRC TECHNICAL PAPER 14   1979   pp91

IRC,INTERNATIONAL REFERENCE CENTRE,
THE HAGUE

The design and construction of a standpost are outlined with
graphical determination of the number of taps and diameter of
service pipe required. Specific detail of taps, valves and drainage
requirements are supported with construction drawings and bill of
quantities for 12 models of standposts.

STANDPOSTS/TAPS/VALVES/DRAINAGE

5114

SMALL COMMUNITY WATER SUPPLIES

IRC TECHNICAL PAPER 18   1981   pp362 + Annex 1-5

IRC,INTERNATIONAL REFERENCE CENTRE
THE HAGUE

Technology for small water supply systems including types of
distribution system and connections are described. Topics covered
include technical design criteria, storage requirements, and
construction details for storage tanks and well as pipe materials
and their selection.

WATER DISTRIBUTION/HOUSE CONNECTIONS/
YARD TAPS/STANDPOSTS/WATER STORAGE/PIPES

5115

A HANDBOOK OF GRAVITY FLOW WATER SYSTEMS FOR
SMALL COMMUNITIES

JORDAN T. 1984   pp224

INTERMEDIATE TECHNOLOGY PUBLICATIONS
LONDON

A practical manual describing design, and construction procedures
for both pipelines and structures required for small water supply
schemes. Sections covered include evaluation and feasibility
studies, surveying, design and selection of system, hydraulic
design as well as pipeline structure construction. The text is
supported by useful data tables, clear diagrams of simple structures
and helpful advice for building systems in difficult and isolated
locations.

PIPES/STANDPOSTS/VALVES/WATER TANKS/
WATER DISTRIBUTION

5116

APPROPRIATE TECHNOLOGY FOR WATER SUPPLY AND
SANITATION VOL 1 TECHNICAL AND ECONOMIC
OPTIONS

KALBERMATTEN J.M.
JULIUS D.S.
GUNNERSON C.G.   1980   pp124

WORLD BANK
WASHINGTON DC

The report presents results and analysis based on field studies as
part of a sanitation study examining household and community
water supply systems, and sullage disposal. Apart from an
evaluation of the technology, both financial and economic
comparisons were made and the impact of health and social factors
assessed. The implications for programme planning including
implementation, and the involvement of institutions and
community participation is examined.

WATER SUPPLY/SULLAGE/COSTS/
COMMUNITY PARTICIPATION

5117

DESIGN GUIDELINES FOR LOW COST WATER AND
SANITATION

LAURIA D.T.   1981   pp24

PAPER PRESENTED AT ASCE MEETING , NEW YORK,
MAY 1981
AMERICAN SOCIETY OF CIVIL ENGINEERS

The paper presents design standards in terms of level of service and optimal resource use to meet these standards. Specific implications of this approach for the design of systems, network costs for water and sanitation and the cost of upgrading are discussed.

STANDPOSTS/PIPES/INDIVIDUAL WATER CONNECTIONS/ MULTI TAP

5118

MANUAL ON WATER TANKS

MABUBA P.B.   1982

Unpublished MSc thesis pp114
LOUGHBOROUGH UNIVERSITY OF TECHNOLOGY

Guidelines and general information on the design and maintenance of concrete water tanks are presented with specific emphasis on structural design (including capacity, costs, materials and joint considerations), construction and maintenance (including leakage and testing).

WATER TANKS/COSTS/MAINTENANCE

5119

WATER SUPPLY FOR RURAL AREAS AND SMALL COMMUNITIES

WAGNER E.C.
LANOIX J.N.   1959

WHO MONOGRAPH SERIES No.42   pp337
WORLD HEALTH ORGANISATION
GENEVA

The development of a water supply programme is described including the installation of various types of systems based on groundwater, and surface water, together with the provision of treatment and distribution. The management requirements of operation and maintenance are also detailed.

WATER SUPPLY/WELLS/HANDPUMPS

5120

MICROCOMPUTER PROGRAMS FOR IMPROVED PLANNING AND DESIGN OF WATER SUPPLY AND WASTE DISPOSAL SYSTEMS

INTERREGIONAL PROJECT INT/81/047   1987

WORLD BANK
WASHINGTON DC

The personal computer program, supported by a user manual enables the hydraulic design and analsis of simple branched and looped water distribution systems to be carried out. Hydraulic

conditions for gravity sewerage can also be analysed. The software is simple to use and requires only a basic understanding of micro computers.

WATER DISTRIBUTION/HYDRAULICS/SEWERAGE/ COMPUTER SOFTWARE

SEE 1102
SEE 1103
SEE 1104
SEE 1105
SEE 1107
SEE 1108
SEE 1109
SEE 1110
SEE 1111
SEE 1112
SEE 1113

5201

THE USE OF PUBLIC RESOURCES FOR WATER SUPPLY AND SANITATION PROJECTS IN DEVELOPING COUNTRIES

BRISCOE J.

AQUA NO3   1987   p137-143
JOURNAL OF THE INTERNATIONAL WATER SUPPLY ASSOCIATION
PERGAMON PRESS
OXFORD

Comparison between limited impact programmes (biomedical) and multiple impact programmes (water and sanitation) to determine which is the most cost effective when limited resources are available together with consideration of the costs and the willingness of beneficiaries to pay.

HEALTH/COSTS

5202

MEASUREMENT OF THE ELASTICITY OF DOMESTIC WATER DEMAND: STUDY OF WATER VENDORS AND THEIR CLIENTS IN URBAN SUDAN

CAIRNCROSS A.M.
KINNEAR J.   1988 pp92

Unpublished report for
OVERSEAS DEVELOPMENT ADMINISTRATION   by
LONDON SCHOOL OF HYGIENE AND TROPICAL MEDICINE

A study of poor urban residents in Khartoum investigating water use, water payments through vendors, benefits and price elasticity of demand. Households paying up to 56% of income for water showed no tendency to use smaller amounts.

WATER USE/TARIFFS/PRICE ELASTICITY

\--

5203

APPLYING LESSONS FROM HOUSING TO MEETING THE CHALLENGE OF WATER AND SANITATION FOR THE URBAN POOR

CAMPBELL T.   1987

JOURNAL OF THE AMERICAN PLANNING ASSOCIATION
VOL.53 (2)   p186-192

This article suggests that a socio-technical strategy is required to reduce the cost of water and sanitation. Lessons from the housing sector are described together with discussion of the ground work required for institutional change which includes changing public utilities attitudes toward low-income settlements, loosening central government control, sharing responsibility with low-income settlements. Specific lessons from Brazilian experience with low-cost sanitation are described.

WATER SUPPLY/COMMUNITY PARTICIPATION/
INSTITUTIONS/SANITATION/BRAZIL

\--

5204

RAINWATER FOR DRINKING IN SRI LANKA

COTTON A.P.

AQUA NO 2 1986 p72-76
JOURNAL OF THE INTERNATIONAL WATER SUPPLY
ASSOCIATION
PERGAMON PRESS
OXFORD

The potential of rainwater as a source of drinking water supply in different climatic zones of Sri Lanka is discussed. In dry zones the storage costs are prohibitive and financial analysis indicates the high cost of this form of water supply even when technologically feasible.

ROOF CATCHMENTS/WATER STORAGE/COSTS/
SRI LANKA

\--

5205

WATER SUPPLY IMPROVEMENTS FOR UPGRADING AREAS WITH SPECIAL REFERENCE TO AUTOMATIC SELF CLOSING TAPS

de KRUIJFF G.J.W.   1979

HOUSING RESEARCH AND DEVELOPMENT UNIT   pp31
UNIVERSITY OF NAIROBI

Description of the 3 main levels of water supply for low-income areas with a comparison of cost is given. The problems of individual supplies are noted, collection of charges, flow restrictions and maintenance. The Fordilla valve (self closing tap) is shown to produce a cost effective solution with a number of advantages over other systems.

WATER SUPPLY/STANDPOSTS/
INDIVIDUAL WATER CONNECTIONS/TAPS/PIPES/COSTS/
COMMUNITY PARTICIPATION/VALVES/KENYA

\--

5206

COSTS FOR SUPPLYING ALTERNATIVE COMMUNITY WATER AND SANITATION SYSTEMS IN BRAZIL

DEMKE K.A.
LAURIA D.T.   1982

JOURNAL OF THE AMERICAN WATER WORKS
ASSOCIATION
VOL 74 (4)   p171-177
COLORADO

The report describes a case study of a small town in Brazil where the cost (including construction, operation and maintenance) of water supply and sanitation were analysed. Levels of service provided and alternative designs of water and sanitation facilities are described. Cost functions were derived for the facilities.

WATER SUPPLY/SANITATION/OPTIONS/COSTS/BRAZIL

\--

5207

SENSITIVITY OF WATER DISTRIBUTION COSTS TO DESIGN AND SERVICE STANDARDS.   A PHILIPPINE CASE STUDY

HEBERT P.V.
YNIGUEZ C. 1986 pp32

UNDP INTERNATIONAL PROJECT INT/81/047
TECHNOLOGY ADVISORY GROUP TECHNICAL NOTE 16
WORLD BANK / UNITED NATIONS DEVELOPMENT
PROGRAMME
WASHINGTON DC

Alternative standards and design criteria for water distribution systems in both small urban and rural areas of the Philippines are compared with the present situation in respect of their impact on system economic costs.

WATER DISTRIBUTION/COSTS/PHILIPPINES

\--

5208

PUBLIC STANDPOST WATER SUPPLY:
A DESIGN MANUAL

IRC TECHNICAL PAPER 14   1979   pp91

IRC,INTERNATIONAL REFERENCE CENTRE
THE HAGUE

The design and construction of a standpost are outlined with
graphical determination of the number of taps and diameter of
service pipe required. Specific detail of taps, valves and drainage
requirements are supported with construction drawings and bill of
quantities for 12 models of standposts.

WATER SUPPLY/STANDPOSTS/COSTS/
COMMUNITY PARTICIPATION/OPERATION/MAINTENANCE

5209

COMMUNITY PIPED WATER SUPPLY SYSTEMS IN
DEVELOPING COUNTRIES: A PLANNING MANUAL

OKUN D.A.
ERNST R.   1987

TECHNICAL PAPER No 60   pp249
WORLD BANK
WASHINGTON DC

This planning manual is intended to be the basis of country
planning manuals for community piped water systems. Important
issues considered include health, economic and social benefits,
environmental and social constraints, technical, economic,
financial, logistical, institutional and socio-cultural factors.
Technical sections included cover water quality, systems capacity,
water source selection, transmission, distribution and treatment as
well as operation and maintenance.

WATER SUPPLY/COSTS/BENEFITS/OPERATION/
MAINTENANCE/WATER DISTRIBUTION

5210

WATER SUPPLY SERVICE FOR THE URBAN POOR: ISSUES

WORLD BANK PUBLIC UTILITIES NOTE 31   1977   pp42

ENERGY, WATER AND TELECOMMUNICATIONS
DEPARTMENT
WORLD BANK
WASHINGTON DC

This paper outlines the issues involved in the choice of an
appropriate water supply system for the urban poor in relation to
the Bank's water supply policy. The issues involved include target
population, types of service, health, supply and distribution,

financing. The role of institutions and community participation is
also discussed.

WATER DISTRIBUTION/COSTS/INSTITUTIONS/
COMMUNITY PARTICIPATION

SEE 1228
SEE 1233
SEE 1204
SEE 6208

5301

OPERATION AND MAINTENANCE OF WATER SUPPLY
AND SANITATION SYSTEMS

GROVER B.   1982 p327-341
in
WATER SUPPLY AND SANITATION IN DEVELOPING
COUNTRIES
SCHILLER E.J.(eds)
DROSTE R.L.   1982

ANN ARBOR SCIENCE
MICHIGAN

Definitions and examples of operation and maintenance systems
are given together with a discussion of the causes and solutions to
operation and maintenance problems, including poor design, lack
of personnel and resources. Ideas for better operation and
maintenance are presented under the headings of money,
management, motivation and manpower.

WATER SUPPLY/OPERATION/MAINTENANCE

5302

ORGANISING MAINTENANCE IN WATER SUPPLY
PROJECT IMPLEMENTATION

HOFKES E.   1984 p3.1-21

2ND AFRICAN WATER TECHNOLOGY CONFERENCE
10-11 TH APRIL 1984
NAIROBI
AFRICAN WATER AND SEWERAGE JOURNAL
REDHILL

Maintenance problems relating to financial and organisational
constraints are described and key considerations in attaining an
effective maintenance program outlined. The management,
financing and organisation of different types of maintenance
system are detailed together with their requirements for manpower,
equipment and records.

WATER SUPPLY/MAINTENANCE

5303

MAINTENANCE FOR HIGH TECHNOLOGY AND LOW
COST SYSTEMS

PICKFORD J.A.   1985 p 5:1-10

ASIAN WATER TECHNOLOGY CONFERENCE   KUALA
LUMPUR NOV 1985
INTERNATIONAL CONFERENCES AND EXHIBITIONS LTD
LONDON

A review of maintenance performance is given including reasons
for failure, including design shortcomings, poor record keeping,
insufficient manpower and the lack of provision of maintenance
systems.

WATER SUPPLY/MAINTENANCE

5304

MAINTENANCE OF WATER AND SANITATION
FACILITIES

SHIPMANN H.   1982

COURSE NOTE SERIES   CN-876   pp19
ECONOMIC DEVELOPMENT INSTITUTE
WORLD BANK
WASHINGTON DC

A review of the four fundamentals of good maintenance as
defined by the terms programmes, personnel, parts and records.
Definitions of maintenance together with the factors affecting
maintenance, economic considerations and criteria for evaluation
are also considered.

MAINTENANCE/WATER SUPPLY/SANITATION

5305

WATER FOR THE WORLD TECHNICAL NOTES RURAL
WATER SUPPLY RWS 1-5

USAID   (undated)

UNITED STATES AGENCY FOR INTERNATIONAL
DEVELOPMENT
WASHINGTON DC

These technical notes include sections on groundwater (covering
design of dug, driven, jetted, bored and cable tool drilled wells,
well construction, testing and installation of aprons and
soakaways). The sections of most interest for urban services
consider community distribution systems, operation and
maintenance and alternative methods of storing water.
Consideration of the storage of groundwater once extracted
includes the design and construction of cisterns, ground and
elevated tanks.

WATER SUPPLY/WELLS/SOAKAWAYS/STANDPOST/
STORAGE/OPERATION/MAINTENANCE/CISTERNS/
WATER TANKS

5306

ASSESSMENT OF THE OPERATIONS AND MAINTENANCE
COMPONENTS OF WATER SUPPLY PROJECTS

WASH TECHNICAL REPORT NO 35   1986   pp90

WATER AND SANITATION FOR HEALTH PROJECT
VIRGINIA

The purpose of this report is to propose a technique for project
planners to analyse the operation and maintenance needs of water
supply projects. Key elements in operation and maintenance are
outlined together with descriptions of the types of water supply
systems in developing countries. Project planning for
maintenance is explained and an operation and maintenance guide
for a supply fed from springs and handpumps presented.

WATER SUPPLY/OPERATION/MAINTENANCE/
HANDPUMPS

SEE 1236

5401

STANDPIPE PLANNING FOR SQUATTERS IN THE URBAN
SUDAN

ANTONIOU J.   1980

WORLD WATER 3 (11) November 1980   p42-45
THOMAS TELFORD
LONDON

A description of urban conditions in Sudan is given including
current standpipe provision and the continuing importance of water
collection. The costs and health problems of water obtained from
vendors is discussed.

WATER SUPPLY/STANDPOSTS/VENDORS/SUDAN

5402

EXPERIENCE WITH LOW COST WATER SUPPLY

CAMPEN R.C.
ENGELSMAN C.M.
MULLIGANIH van   1984   p205-208

WATER AND SANITATION IN ASIA AND THE PACIFIC
10th WEDC CONFERENCE   SINGAPORE
LOUGHBOROUGH UNIVERSITY OF TECHNOLOGY

Details of the IKK water supply concept which entails the provision of storage tanks at the delivery end of the system are given. This results in reduced peak flow, hence smaller diameter supply pipes.   Other aspects covered include design, implementation, operation and maintenance, cost recovery and community participation.

WATER SUPPLY/WATER STORAGE/OPERATION/
MAINTENANCE/COMMUNITY PARTICIPATION/COSTS/
INDONESIA

5403

PLACING WATER SUPPLY AND SEWER MAINS IN THE
SAME TRENCH
EXPERIENCES DERIVED FROM A STUDY IN AMMAN
JORDAN

ENVIRONMENTAL SANITATION REVIEWS NO 15   1984
pp46

ENVIRONMENTAL SANITATION INFORMATION CENTRE
ASIAN INSTITUTE OF TECHNOLOGY
BANGKOK

The joint development of a sewer and water supply system is described in Amman. Consideration is given to the cost advantages, particular pipeline construction practices, and technologies based on U.S. regulations, and the assessment of any contamination. System pressures, leakage and the use of a septic tank system are also discussed.

WATER MAINS/SEWERS/SEPTIC TANKS/ECONOMICS/
JORDAN

5404

WATER FOR THE URBAN POOR

FRIEDLANDER, PAUL

WATERLINES, VOL 9, NO 1, JULY 1990, p6-8

The article describes a successful project for urban water supply, developed by the Honduran Government and UNICEF.

WATER SUPPLY/COMMUNITY PARTICIPATION

5405

NATIONAL PROGRAMME FOR WATER SUPPLY AND
SANITATION

GOVERNMENT OF THE MALDIVES 1985 pp62

This review of water and sanitation in the Maldives includes sections on the country and its people, the existing facilities and methods of water supply and sanitation used, sector policies, and construction materials and methods. Appendices covering the

design and costs of systems are provided.

WATER SUPPLY/WELLS/WATER TANKS/STANDPOSTS/
SANITATION/IMPLEMENTATION/COSTS/MALDIVES

5406

JUBA AREA WATER SUPPLY STUDY   SUDAN

NICHOLS P.   1983 pp83

LOW INCOME HOUSING UNIT
REGIONAL MINISTRY OF HOUSING AND PUBLIC
UTILITIES
JUBA

This evaluation of the Juba water supply system includes a description of the physical location, current and projected water supply usage, existing standposts and borewells and the extent of private sector water deliveries. Existing public water points are evaluated and recommendations for management and maintenance improvements presented, along with suggestions on extensions to the existing supply.

WATER SUPPLY/STANDPOSTS/MAINTENANCE/VENDORS/
SUDAN

5407

URBAN WATER SUPPLY AND SANITATION FEASIBILITY
STUDY FOR MBALE UGANDA

PARKMAN CONSULTANTS LTD 1981 SECTIONS A-J

PARKMAN CONSULTANTS LTD
LIVERPOOL

Current water sources, their treatment and distribution are outlined together with the extent of existing septic tanks and pit latrines. A survey of low-cost sanitation systems including customs is reported. Proposals for improvement include surface water drainage and septic tank and low-cost sanitation systems including VIP, aqua privy, pour flush, and pit latrines with sullage disposal and washing slabs. Likely costs and necessary institutional structures are detailed.

WATER SUPPLY/DRAINAGE/SANITATION OPTIONS/
SULLAGE/WASHING SLABS/COSTS/UGANDA

5408

PIPED WATER SUPPLY TO LOW INCOME HOUSING

POSTMA S.F. 1983

WATER SUPPLY VOL 1 [4] p222
INTERNATIONAL WATER SUPPLY ASSOCIATION
LONDON

A study of six cities in Indonesia shows a clear preference for individual connections over public taps even in low-income areas. Metered supply to low-income households is considered with comparative costs of public taps versus individual connections outlined.

WATER SUPPLY/PUBLIC TAPS/
INDIVIDUAL WATER CONNECTIONS/COSTS/INDONESIA

5409

THE DEVELOPMENT OF WATER SUPPLY IN INDONESIA

SCHALEKAMP M.   1985

AQUA No 1   1985   p10
THE JOURNAL OF THE INTERNATIONAL WATER SUPPLY
ASSOCIATION
PERGAMON PRESS
OXFORD

This overview of the urban and rural water supplies of Indonesia is supported with tabulated water supply and demand tables. Storage methods employed by IKK, illustrated with drawings are discussed.

WATER SUPPLY/WATER STORAGE/INDONESIA

SEE 1403
SEE 1406
SEE 1407
SEE 1410
SEE 1409
SEE 1414
SEE 1412
SEE 1420
SEE 1421
SEE 1422
SEE 1424
SEE 1426
SEE 1427

Section 6. SANITATION

6101

WASTEWATER TREATMENT AND EXCRETA DISPOSAL IN
DEVELOPING COUNTRIES

BAUMANN W.
KARPE H.J.   1980 pp180

INSTITUTE OF ENVIRONMENTAL PROTECTION
UNIVERSITY OF DORTMUND
GERMAN APPROPRIATE TECHNOLOGY EXCHANGE
ESCHBORN

This manual gives planning and practical advice in respect of a
wide range of technologies including pit latrines, aqua privies,
septic tanks, communal facilities, stabilisation ponds, bucket and
vault systems. The provision of either open channels or pipes for
wastewater drainage is also discussed.

PIT LATRINES/AQUA PRIVY/COMMUNAL LATRINES/
STABILISATION PONDS/SEPTIC TANKS/
BUCKET LATRINES/VAULT/CHANNELS/PIPES

6102

THE CHOICE BETWEEN SEPTIC TANKS AND SEWERS IN
TROPICAL DEVELOPING COUNTRIES

BRADLEY R.M.   1983

PUBLIC HEALTH ENGINEER VOL 11 (1)   p20-28
JOURNAL OF THE INSTITUTION OF PUBLIC HEALTH
ENGINEERS
LONDON

Health risks from overloaded sewers are described and septic tank
and soakaway layouts described. System design is outlined based
on percolation tests and estimates of site requirements. Costs of
sewers and septic tanks are compared.

SEPTIC TANK/SOAKAWAY/PERCOLATION/COST/
SEWERAGE

6103

SANITATION FOR DEVELOPING COUNTRIES

CARROLL R.F.   1982

OVERSEAS BUILDING NOTE No 189   pp11
BUILDING RESEARCH ESTABLISHMENT
WATFORD

This review of sanitation systems outlines their characteristics and
describes problems such as health nuisance and the pollution of the
soil.

POLLUTION/BUCKET LATRINES/OVERHUNG LATRINES/
PIT LATRINES/BOREHOLE LATRINES/VIP/
COMPOST LATRINES/POUR FLUSH LATRINES/VAULTS/
SEPTIC TANK/AQUA PRIVY

6104

SHALLOW SEWERS
IDEAL FOR HIGH DENSITY LOW INCOME AREAS

ENFO VOL 9 (2)   1987 p3

ENVIRONMENTAL SANITATION INFORMATION CENTRE
ASIAN INSTITUTE OF TECHNOLOGY
BANGKOK

Details of shallow sewers in preference to pit and pour flush
systems are given together with their advantages, costs and
practical details of the system.

SHALLOW SEWERS/PIT LATRINES/
POUR FLUSH LATRINES/COSTS

6105

SEWERAGE & SEWAGE TREATMENT

ESCRITT L.B.
HAWORTH W.D.   1984   pp539

JOHN WILEY
CHICHESTER

Principles of drainage and sewerage including the construction and
location of surface drains and sewers are discussed. Topics
covered include flow in sewers, the design of storage and
soakaways for surface water and the construction of sewers
(covering material types, protection, and sewer appurtenances
such as manholes and soakaways).

SURFACE DRAINS/SOAKAWAYS/SEWERS

6106

ALTERNATIVE SANITARY WASTE REMOVAL SYSTEMS
FOR LOW INCOME URBAN AREAS IN DEVELOPING
COUNTRIES

HANSEN J.A.
THERKELSEN H.   1978   pp143

POLYTEKNIK FORLAG
DENMARK

This report includes sections on the historical development of
sanitation systems and a general evaluation of criteria and
assumptions used in the selected study area. Technologies

assumptions used in the selected study area. Technologies considered include full sewerage, aqua privy with sewers, vault and vacuum truck and bucket latrine. A comparative evaluation is presented based on service levels achieved and total costs of each alternative.

SEWERAGE/AQUA PRIVY/VAULTS/BUCKET LATRINES/
COSTS

6107

APPROPRIATE SANITATION ALTERNATIVES
A PLANNING AND DESIGN MANUAL
WORLD BANK STUDIES IN WATER SUPPLY AND
SANITATION

KALBERMATTEN J.M.
JULIUS D.S.
GUNNERSON C.G.
MARA D.D.   1982   pp160

JOHN HOPKINS UNIVERSITY PRESS
BALTIMORE

The problems of establishing appropriate sanitation systems are explored with reference to the constraints of upgrading and planning and the limitations of the alternative technologies. Detail is given on the design costs, upgrading alternatives, maintenance requirements and construction and operation of a range of technologies including pit latrines, VIP, pour flush, aqua privy, septic tank soakaways, drainfields, and communal systems.

PIT LATRINES/MAINTENANCE/
SANITATION UPGRADING/AQUA PRIVY/SEPTIC TANKS/
SOAKAWAYS/COSTS/DRAINFIELDS/
COMMUNAL LATRINES/VIP LATRINES/
POUR FLUSH LATRINES

6108

THE RISK OF GROUNDWATER POLLUTION BY ON SITE
SANITATION IN DEVELOPING COUNTRIES: A
LITERATURE REVIEW

LEWIS W.J
FOSTER S.S.D.
DRASAR B.S.   1980 pp79

IRCWD REPORT NO 01/82
INTERNATIONAL REFERENCE CENTRE FOR WASTE
DISPOSAL
DUEBENDORF

This literature review covers the principles of pollutant movement and attenuation within the ground, applied field investigations of pollutant movement with case histories and nitrate pollution of groundwater. The implications for on site sanitation are discussed.

ON SITE SANITATION/GROUNDWATER POLLUTION

6109

SANITATION WITHOUT SEWERS - THE AQUA PRIVY

MANN H.T.   1976 p1-6

WATER RESEARCH COUNCIL
STEVENAGE
OVERSEAS BUILDING NOTE 168
BUILDING RESEARCH ESTABLISHMENT

This review of sanitation in sewerless areas also provides details of modifications to aqua privies including connections to an evapotranspiration bed, a double chamber aqua privy connected to a seepage pit, and an oil drum privy connected to a seepage pit.

AQUA PRIVY/SEEPAGE PIT/EVAPOTRANSPIRATION BED

6110

RATIONAL DESIGN OF SEPTIC TANKS IN WARM
CLIMATES

MARA D.D.
SINNATAMBY G.S.   1986

THE PUBLIC HEALTH ENGINEER VOL 14 (4)   p49-55
INSTITUTION OF PUBLIC HEALTH ENGINEERS
STERLING PUBLICATIONS
LONDON

A rational design including sedimentation and digestion of settleable solids is discussed in relation to current design criteria and performance of the system. Detail on the storage of digested sludge and the design of the facilities are supported with tables on sludge accumulation, temperature effects on the sludge, and retention times.

SEPTIC TANK/SLUDGE

6111

THE DESIGN OF VIP LATRINES

MARA D.D.   1984

UNDP INTREGPROINT/81/047
TECHNOLOGY ADVISORY GROUP TECHNICAL NOTE 13
pp73
WORLD BANK
WASHINGTON DC

The design and construction of VIPs is detailed in terms of subsoil conditions, system constraints, operational considerations and individual system components and illustrated with a design example. Case studies describe construction approaches (including a sketch of the design)as adopted in Zimbabwe, Botswana, Tanzania, Ghana, and Brazil with alternative construction material costs presented for Zimbabwe.

VIP LATRINES/COSTS/ZIMBABWE/BOTSWANA/
TANZANIA/GHANA/BRAZIL

6112

LOW COST SYSTEMS OFTEN BEATS SEWERS

MOES W.
ZWAGG R.R.   1984

WORLD WATER   VOL7 (9)   p56-57
THOMAS TELFORD
LONDON

Sewers are compared with pour flush and septic tanks in both
suburban and urban areas of Bangladesh. A case study in the
Chittagong area, compares a range of options including pour flush,
sewers, vault and septic tanks. Selection criteria based on water
service levels, population density, soil and water table interfaces,
socio-cultural and financial aspects are detailed.

POUR FLUSH LATRINES/SEPTIC TANKS/SEWERAGE/
VAULTS/BANGLADESH/FINANCE

6113

VENTILATED IMPROVED PIT LATRINES:
ZIMBABWEAN BRICK DESIGN

MORGAN P.R.
MARA D.D.   1985

TECHNOLOGY ADVISORY GROUP DISCUSSION PAPER 1
pp47
WORLD BANK
WASHINGTON DC

This report describes a move in Zimbabwe to brick built
superstructures due to the expense of ferrocement and scarcity of
wood for mud/wattle construction. Various designs are reviewed
in terms of their maintenance requirements and costs.

VIP LATRINES/MAINTENANCE/COSTS/ZIMBABWE

6114

THE PERFORMANCE OF POUR FLUSH TOILETS: A CASE
STUDY IN AN INDIAN CONTEXT

NIYOGI S.
DAS D.K.   1984

WATER AND SANITATION IN ASIA AND THE PACIFIC
10th WEDC CONFERENCE SINGAPORE p192-195
LOUGHBOROUGH UNIVERSITY OF TECHNOLOGY

This paper describes an investigation into subsoil effluent dispersal
with discussion of the rate of sludge accumulation, the problems of
odour and other nuisances, and costs. Drawings of an experimental
pour flush latrine are appended.

POUR FLUSH LATRINES/SLUDGE/EFFLUENT/INDIA

6115

VENTILATED IMPROVED DOUBLE PIT LATRINES - A
CONSTRUCTION MANUAL FOR BOTSWANA

NOSTRAND van J.
WILSON J.G.   1983

GOVERNMENT OF BOTSWANA
TECHNOLOGY ADVISORY GROUP TECHNICAL NOTE 3
pp47
WORLD BANK
WASHINGTON DC

This manual describes the principles of the VIDP latrine together
with advice on construction, operation and maintenance. The
importance of inspection during the latrines construction as well as
monitoring during operation are discussed. Appendices contain
working drawings and design details.

VIDP LATRINES/OPERATION/MAINTENANCE/BOTSWANA

6116

LOW VOLUME W C SYSTEMS:
A DEVELOPMENT PROJECT IN INDIA

OLSSON E.   1988

RESEARCH REPORT TN4 pp96
NATIONAL SWEDISH INSTITUTE FOR BUILDING
RESEARCH
GAVLE

This project report describes project development and trial design,
together with details of the pans, traps and the cistern. The results
of the field trials are discussed and recommendations made.

LOW VOLUME FLUSH W.C./INDIA

6117

DEVELOPMENT OF THE AQUA PRIVY FOR URBAN
SANITATION

OLUWANDE P.A.   1975

WATER, WASTE AND HEALTH IN HOT COUNTRIES
2nd WEDC CONFERENCE LOUGHBOROUGH p109-117
LOUGHBOROUGH UNIVERSITY OF TECHNOLOGY

Common disposal methods in developing countries including
open defecation, bucket and pit latrine are described and
contrasted with the aqua privy. A cost comparison of the aqua

privy with septic tank and pit latrine options is included. Details
on the construction and operation of individual and communal
(comfort station) aqua privies are given.

AQUA PRIVY/COMMUNAL LATRINES/OPERATION

6118

THE DESIGN OF SMALL BORE SEWERS SYSTEMS

OTIS R.J.
MARA D.D.   1985

TECHNOLOGY ADVISORY GROUP TECHNICAL NOTE 14
pp52
WORLD BANK
WASHINGTON DC

Small bore sewer systems and their component parts are described
in terms of their applicability to developing countries. Design
criteria and construction and maintenance guidelines are presented
for interceptor tanks, appurtenances and the various wastewater
treatment options. Case studies from Zambia, Australia, Nigeria
and U.S.A. are included. Interceptor and small bore sewer design
examples are detailed in the annexes.

SMALL BORE SEWERS/MAINTENANCE/ZAMBIA/
INTERCEPTOR TANKS/NIGERIA/COSTS/WASTEWATER

6119

THE OXFAM SANITATION UNIT

OXFAM/MARSTON JULY 1975

PREPARED BY
HOWARD J.
LLOYD B.
WEBBER D.

OXFAM
OXFORD

The requirements for use and applications for the portable
sanitation unit are described. Each part of the package including
special features and site choice is outlined. Details of latrine
assembly, soakaway construction and operation, installation and
desludging of the sewage containment tanks are given.

SOAKAWAYS/COMMUNAL LATRINES

6120

REDUCED COST SEWERAGE FOR DEVELOPING
COUNTRIES

PICKFORD J.A.
REED R.A.
VINES M.   1989   pp44

Unpublished report by
WATER ENGINEERING AND DEVELOPMENT CENTRE
LOUGHBOROUGH UNIVERSITY OF TECHNOLOGY
for OVERSEAS DEVELOPMENT ADMINISTRATION
LONDON

A literature survey of information concerning reduced cost
sewerage. Technical and non-technical issues are investigated with
design, operational and cost experience from ten countries.

SEWERAGE/MAINTENANCE/COSTS/PAKISTAN/
COLOMBIA/BRAZIL/INDONESIA/BOLIVIA/
ZAMBIA

6121

THE DESIGN OF SEPTIC TANKS AND AQUA PRIVIES

PICKFORD J.A.   1980

OVERSEAS BUILDING NOTE 187 pp12.
BUILDING RESEARCH ESTABLISHMENT
WATFORD

The note covers design objectives and factors affecting
performance with details on the processes in the tank, tank sizing
and examples, materials to be used and methods of construction
and maintenance requirements.

SEPTIC TANKS/AQUA PRIVIES/MAINTENANCE

6122

SEPTIC TANK AND SEPTIC SYSTEMS

POLPRASERT C.
RAJPUT, V.S.
DONALDSON, D.
VIRARAGHAVAN, T.   1982

ENVIRONMENTAL SANITATION REVIEWS No 7/8   pp110
ASIAN INSTITUTE OF TECHNOLOGY
BANGKOK

This review includes descriptions of the characteristics of
wastewater and the internal processes in the tank. Topics covered
include tank design and construction (shape, size,
compartmentation, ventilation, and materials), operation and
maintenance, system performance, disposal of the effluent (via
filters, evapotranspiration beds or sub-surface disposal) and any
environmental effects.

SEPTIC TANK/OPERATION/MAINTENANCE/EFFLUENT/
EVAPOTRANSPIRATION BEDS/SEPTAGE

6123

LOW COST TECHNOLOGY OPTIONS FOR SANITATION
STATE-OF-THE-ART REVIEW AND ANNOTATED
BIBLIOGRAPHY

RYBCZYNSKI W.
POLPRASERT C.
MCGARRY M.   1982   pp184

WORLD BANK
WASHINGTON DC

A comprehensive technology review and bibliography describing
alternative approaches to collection, treatment, reuse and disposal
of human wastes. Emphasis on technology but institutional,
behavioural and health related aspects are also considered.

SANITATION OPTIONS

6124

THE TOILET PAPERS

RYN van der S   1978   pp124

CAPRA PRESS
CALIFORNIA

Based on USA experience wastewater use is examined with
consideration of septic tanks and subsurface drainfields including
soakaway, filters and treatment tank and the opportunities for
modified household plumbing. The problems of using sullage
and greywater in the garden are discussed and necessary
precautions suggested.

SULLAGE/SEPTIC TANKS/SOAKAWAYS/USA

6125

WET METHODS OF EXCRETA DISPOSAL

DROSTE R.L. p157-176
in
WATER SUPPLY AND SANITATION IN DEVELOPING
COUNTRIES

SCHILLER E.J. (eds)
DROSTE R.L.   1982

ANN ARBOR SCIENCE
MICHIGAN

Design and operation together with socio-cultural and health
aspects of the aqua privy and septic tank are discussed. Detail is
included on methods of operation, sizing of tanks, opportunity for
communal toilets, water seal and solids problems, and effluent
disposal in leaching fields, or evapotranspiration beds.

AQUA PRIVY/SEPTIC TANKS/LEACH FIELDS/
EVAPOTRANSPIRATION BEDS/COMMUNAL LATRINES

6126

SEPTIC TANK DESIGN, CONSTRUCTION AND
MAINTENANCE PRACTICES

SHETTY M.S.   1971 D5 p1-21

IN: SEMINAR ON WATER SUPPLY AND SANITATION
PROBLEMS IN URBAN AREAS   VOL II
PUBLIC HEALTH ENGINEERING DIVISION
THE INSTITUTION OF ENGINEERS   INDIA

Design criteria such as tank capacity, detention period, sludge and
scum storage and physical characteristics including shape, depth
and compartmentation are discussed. Other topics covered include
effluent disposal, maintenance including desludging, sludge
disposal and disinfection, siting of the tank, and absorption drains.

SEPTIC TANKS/SLUDGE/ABSORPTION DRAINS/
MAINTENANCE

6127

DESIGN OF SMALL DIAMETER VARIABLE GRADE
GRAVITY SEWERS

SIMMONS J.D.
NEWMAN J.O.   1984

AGRICULTURAL HANDBOOK NO 626 pp13
UNITED STATES DEPARTMENT OF AGRICULTURE
MARYLAND

The use, operational characteristics and design considerations of
2" diameter variable grade sewers with modified septic tanks as
interceptor tanks are discussed.

SMALL BORE SEWERAGE/SEPTIC TANKS/
INTERCEPTOR TANKS

6128

GOODBYE TO THE FLUSH TOILET

STONER C.H.   1977   p285

RODALE PRESS
PA USA

Sanitation practices to save water are described in the USA. Detail
is given on greywater volume and quality, treatment options
including pretreatment filters, and disposal in seepage beds,
trenches or surface disposal. An owner built system is described.

SANITATION/SULLAGE/SEEPAGE BEDS/USA

6129

THE DESIGN OF SHALLOW SEWER SYSTEMS

UNCHS 1986   pp87
HS/100/86/E

UNITED NATIONS CENTRE FOR HUMAN SETTLEMENTS
NAIROBI

Characteristics of shallow sewers including their advantages and
methods of operation are discussed. Design criteria and
specifications are presented together with recommendations on
planning and implementation including construction and
maintenance. Project costs and affordability are detailed for a
number of case studies.

SHALLOW SEWERS/COSTS

6130

WATER FOR THE WORLD TECHNICAL NOTES
SANITATION. USAID SAN 1-3 (undated)

UNITED STATES AGENCY FOR INTERNATIONAL
DEVELOPMENT
WASHINGTON DC

Methods for excreta and wastewater disposal are described, with
details of the design, construction, operation and maintenance of
pit latrines, aqua privies, bucket, septic tanks, sewers,
soakaways and sumps. Methods of solid waste management are
also covered under the headings of design, operation and
maintenance of landfill and solid waste collection systems.

PIT LATRINES/AQUA PRIVIES/BUCKET LATRINES/
SEPTIC TANKS/SEWERS/SOAKAWAYS/OPERATION/
MAINTENANCE/SOLID WASTE/LANDFILL

6131

A SYSTEM OF SANITATION FOR LOW COST
HIGH DENSITY HOUSING

VINCENT L.J.
ALGIE W.E.
MARIAS G. Van R.   1961   p135-172

PROCEEDINGS OF A SYMPOSIUM ON HYGIENE AND
SANITATION IN RELATION TO HOUSING
CCTA/WHO
NIAMEY NIGER

Sanitation systems in central Africa are described including pit
latrines, aqua privies, bucket latrines and water-borne sewerage.
Costs and design of the self-topping communal aqua privy with
stabilisation pond are detailed.

AQUA PRIVY/WASTEWATER/SHALLOW SEWERS/

ZAMBIA/STABILISATION PONDS/PIT LATRINES/
BUCKET LATRINES

6132

LOW COST UNCONVENTIONAL SEWERAGE

VINES, MARCUS
REED, BOB

WATERLINES, VOL 9, NO 1, JULY 1990, p26-29

Drawing on experience with unconventional sewerage systems in
Brazil and Pakistan, the article discusses both the technical aspects
of unconventional sewerage and issues related to affordability.

SEWERAGE/SHALLOW SEWERS/BRAZIL/PAKISTAN

6133

LOW VOLUME FLUSH WC DESIGN

WAKELIN R.H.M.
SWAFFIELD J.A.
BOCARRO R.A.   1987 p37-40

RURAL WATER AND ENGINEERING DEVELOPMENT IN
AFRICA
13th WEDC CONFERENCE MALAWI
LOUGHBOROUGH UNIVERSITY OF TECHNOLOGY

An approach to the problem of low water use design is presented
in terms of such variables as trap volume, water seal depth, cistern
to bowl distribution. Site evaluation in Botswana and Lesotho is
described together with the effects of septic tanks and sewerage.

WC/SEPTIC TANKS/SEWERAGE/BOTSWANA/
LESOTHO

6134

THE EFFECTS OF WC DISCHARGE GEOMETRY ON THE
TRANSPORT OF SOLIDS IN INTERNAL DRAINAGE
SYSTEMS

WAKELIN R.H.M.
UUJAMHAN E.J.S. 1979

THE PUBLIC HEALTH ENGINEER VOL 7 (4) p170-175
INSTITUTION OF PUBLIC HEALTH ENGINEERS
STERLING PUBLICATIONS
LONDON

Experimental results are presented which investigate the transport
and deposition of solid matter within waste pipes. The effect of
pipe bends and alignments are discussed and recommendations
appropriate for building drainage systems are made.

SEWERAGE/HOUSE SEWERS

6135

DESIGN AND CONSTRUCTION OF SANITARY AND
STORM SEWERS

WATER POLLUTION CONTROL FEDERATION
MANUAL OF PRACTICE NO 9   1980

AMERICAN SOCIETY OF CIVIL ENGINEERS

This manual covers the technical issues involved in the design and
construction of sewers with the topics covered including
organisation and administration, site survey and investigation,
quantities of sewage and stormwater, structural and hydraulic
design of systems, appurtenances and material selection.
Pumping stations are also considered.

STORMWATER OPTIONS/SEWERAGE

6136

THE MINIMISATION OF MICROBIOLOGICAL HAZARDS
ASSOCIATED WITH LATRINE WASTES

WHEELER D.
CARROLL R.F.   1989

WATER SCIENCE AND TECHNOLOGY VOL 21 (3) p35-42
PERGAMON PRESS
OXFORD

Results are reported of the analysis of sludge from latrine wastes
using the faecal bacteria Ascaris, Taenia, Schistosoma and human
enteric viruses as indicator organisms. Comparisons of sludge at
least one year old with sludge less than one year old confirmed the
importance of long term sludge storage to reduce hazardous
organisms.

ON SITE SANITATION/HEALTH/SLUDGE

6137

WASTEWATER STABILISATION PONDS
PRINCIPALS OF PLANNING AND PRACTICE

WHO EMRO TECHNICAL PUBLICATION 10   1987   pp138

WORLD HEALTH ORGANISATION
EASTERN MEDITERRANEAN REGIONAL OFFICE
ALEXANDRIA

Climatic, physical and chemical factors affecting treatment in the
ponds are discussed. Principles of design and construction, and
methods of pond operation, maintenance and management are
outlined.

STABILISATION PONDS/OPERATION/MAINTENANCE

6138

DISPOSAL OF COMMUNITY WASTEWATER

WHO TECHNICAL REPORT 541 1974 pp72
WORLD HEALTH ORGANISATION
GENEVA

Health and environmental aspects of wastewater collection and
disposal are considered together with cultural and socio-economic
aspects. Technical problems of collection and disposal are
discussed within the context of management, planning,
organisation and administration with conclusions and
recommendations presented.

WASTEWATER/COLLECTION/DISPOSAL

6139

WASTE STABILISATION PONDS

GLOYNA E.F.

WHO MONOGRAPH SERIES 60 1971 pp175
WORLD HEALTH ORGANISATION
GENEVA

This general description of pond types, their operation and history
of development includes data on a worldwide survey of pond use
and the characteristics of the influent wastewater. Details of
process design included, consider the layout of facultative,
anaerobic and aerobic ponds and relevant design
recommendations as well as disease control and the operation of
the facilities.

STABILISATION PONDS/OPERATION

SEE 1103
SEE 1104
SEE 1105
SEE 1107
SEE 1108
SEE 1109
SEE 1110
SEE 1111
SEE 1112
SEE 1113
SEE 5104
SEE 5117

6201

SEPTAGE COLLECTION SYSTEM ECONOMICS

BASHER A.
SHAHALAM M.   1986

WATER AND SANITATION AT MID DECADE
12th WEDC CONFERENCE CALCUTTA p104-107

LOUGHBOROUGH UNIVERSITY OF TECHNOLOGY

The economics of individual on site septic tanks, with private truck collection, but public disposal points are presented. Operation and management of septage are discussed and system capital costs detailed.

JORDAN/OPERATION/MANAGEMENT/SEPTIC TANKS/
COSTS/SEPTAGE

6202

TECHNOLOGY OPTIONS FOR LOW COST SANITATION IN
DEVELOPING COUNTRIES

BHUNIA A.K.   1982 p1-3

JOURNAL OF THE INSTITUTE OF ENGINEERS INDIA
ENVIRONMENTAL ENGINEERING DIVISION VOL 63 (1)

Some of the options for improved water supply and sanitation in India are discussed. Economically, socially and environmentally appropriate solutions are sought.

POUR FLUSH LATRINES/WATER SUPPLY/INDIA/
ECONOMICS/COSTS

6203

BRINGING THE TWIN PIT LATRINE TO BOTSWANA

BUILDING RESEARCH ESTABLISHMENT 1982

WATERLINES VOL 1(1) p18-19
INTERMEDIATE TECHNOLOGY PUBLICATIONS
LONDON

Details of experimental work carried out by the BRE and the Botswana government are outlined. Issues discussed include space restrictions, the emptying routine, operational problems including draining water into the pit and financing.

VIDP LATRINES/BOTSWANA/OPERATION

6204

BUFFER ZONES FOR SEWAGE TREATMENT PLANTS IN
DEVELOPING COUNTRIES

ENFO VOL 9 (3) 1987 p2-4

ENVIRONMENTAL SANITATION INFORMATION CENTRE
ASIAN INSTITUTE OF TECHNOLOGY
BANGKOK

An examination of the preferred distances between treatment plants and residential/industrial sites. The paper considers odour, vectors, noise and aesthetics and gives guidelines to minimise the effects on the environment.

SEWAGE TREATMENT/ENVIRONMENTAL BUFFER ZONES

6205

ALTERNATIVE SANITATION TECHNOLOGIES FOR
URBAN AREAS IN AFRICA

FEACHEM R.G.
MARA D.D.
IWUGO K.O.   1979

PUBLIC UTILITY NOTE 22   pp186
WORLD BANK
WASHINGTON DC

Various excreta disposal systems in Africa are compared with respect to their costs, technical constraints, opportunity for upgrading and the interaction between water, sullage and sanitation. Guidelines on selection are made from among systems which include pit, compost, and bucket latrines and aqua privies.

PIT LATRINES/COMPOST LATRINES/BUCKET LATRINES/
AQUA PRIVY/SULLAGE/COSTS

6206

APPROPRIATE SANITATION ALTERNATIVES
A TECHNICAL AND ECONOMIC APPRAISAL

KALBERMATTEN J.M.
JULIUS D.S.
GUNNERSON C.G.   1982   pp115

WORLD BANK STUDIES IN WATER SUPPLY AND
SANITATION I
JOHNS HOPKINS UNIVERSITY PRESS
BALTIMORE

Technical and environmental assessment of sanitation systems including an economic comparison and consideration of public health and socio-economic factors. Topics covered include planning and project development (community participation and implementation).

SANITATION OPTIONS/ECONOMICS/
COMMUNITY PARTICIPATION/INSTITUTIONS

6207

SANITATION FACILITIES FOR SLUMS & RURAL AREAS

MAJUMBER N.   1975   pp24

NATIONAL ENVIRONMENTAL ENGINEERING RESEARCH
INSTITUTE
NAGPUR

A review of sanitation for slum areas including WC's communal latrines and individual latrines. Estimated costs are given.

W C/COMMUNAL LATRINES/INDIA

6208

APPROPRIATE SANITATION FOR URBAN AREAS

NIELSEN J.H.
KASS J.C.   1980   pp138

COWI CONSULT
CONSULTING ENGINEERS AND PLANNERS
VIRUM

This report reviews appropriate sanitation technologies for urban
areas and investigates the problems of financing by the
beneficiaries. Priorities for infrastructure development,
recommendations on the distribution of investments throughout
each sector, and minimum standards for water, sanitation, roads
and surface drainage are presented.

Appropriate solutions such as standposts, single and multiple taps,
sullage, refuse collection stormwater and sanitation are described
together with alternative technology options and costs. Project
appraisal including economic analysis is also discussed.

SANITATION OPTIONS/OPERATION/MAINTENANCE/
COSTS/WATER SUPPLY/ROADS/SURFACE DRAINS/
TAPS/STANDPOSTS/SULLAGE/SOLID WASTE/
STORMWATER OPTIONS

6209

SANITATION IN DEVELOPING COUNTRIES

PACEY A. (ED)   1978   pp238

JOHN WILEY
CHICHESTER

This general text defines the problem of sanitation including
availability of systems in a developing country context. The
appropriate choice of technology from among sewerage, aqua
privies, pit latrines, bucket and vaults etc. is discussed with regard
to the urban poor and social factors relating to the technology, for
example ease of operation and maintenance.

SEWERAGE/AQUA PRIVY/PIT LATRINES/
BUCKET LATRINES/VAULTS/OPERATION/MAINTENANCE

6210

A MONITORING AND EVALUATION MANUAL FOR LOW
COST SANITATION PROGRAMS IN INDIA

PARLATO R.   1984

TECHNOLOGY ADVISORY GROUP TECHNICAL NOTE 12

pp80
WORLD BANK / UNDP
WASHINGTON DC

A manual to help identify the potential problems in monitoring and
evaluation of low-cost systems in India. Technological, financial,
administrative and socio-economic factors are considered together
with the requirements and problems of monitoring and
implementation. Attention is given to pour flush systems.

POUR FLUSH LATRINES/FINANCE/INDIA

6211

SULABH SHAUCHALAYA
HAND FLUSH WATER SEAL LATRINES

PATHAK B. 1981 pp104

SULABH INTERNATIONAL
CALCUTTA

The removal of the "scavengers" in India and the introduction of a
water seal latrine is described together with progress on the
adoption of the system in different Indian states. Details are given
on the latrine's advantages, its construction and the filling rates of
the pits.

POUR FLUSH LATRINES/INDIA

6212

PLANNING AND DESIGN OF LARGE SCALE POUR FLUSH
PROGRAMMES IN URBAN AREAS

ROY A.K. 1982 pp24

IN: PROCEEDINGS OF A SEMINAR ON THE
IMPLEMENTATION OF LOW COST SANITATION
PROGRAMMES IN TANZANIA
ARUSHA INTERNATIONAL CONFERENCE CENTRE
ARDHI INSTITUTE, MINISTRY OF LANDS, HOUSING AND
URBAN

A demonstration project of pour flush latrines is described with
details of the inputs which included evaluation programmes, and
organisational, financial and managerial reviews. Also discussed is
the optimisation of the technology, institutional requirements, and
construction and financial aspects.

POUR FLUSH LATRINES/FINANCE/INDIA

6213

ON-SITE WASTEWATER MANAGEMENT - NORTH
AMERICAN EXPERIENCE AND POSSIBLE LESSONS FOR
INDIA AND OTHER DEVELOPING COUNTRIES

VIRARAGHAVAN, T
BISWAS, N

INTERNATIONAL JOURNAL OF DEVELOPMENT
TECHNOLOGY, 1986, VOL 4, pt 2, p99-109

The authors consider that the existence of an effective
organisational (management) entity, undertaking the installation,
operation and maintenance of on-site wastewater systems, is
essential to the success of such systems.

MANAGEMENT/USA/WASTEWATER

6214

EXCRETA DISPOSAL FOR RURAL AREAS AND SMALL
COMMUNITIES

WAGNER E.C.
LANOIX J.N.   1958

WHO MONOGRAPH SERIES NO 39   pp187
WORLD HEALTH ORGANISATION
GENEVA

A range of disposal methods are described including pit latrines
(simple, aqua privy and water seal) and water carried methods
such as septic tanks.

PIT LATRINES/AQUA PRIVY/POUR FLUSH LATRINES/
SEPTIC TANKS

6215

ECONOMIC AND AFFORDABILITY ANALYSIS OF
SANITATION ALTERNATIVES FOR SELF HELP HOUSING
AREAS IN BOTSWANA

WASH FIELD REPORT NO 148   1986   pp120

WATER AND SANITATION FOR HEALTH PROJECT
VIRGINIA

Background to the analysis includes a description of the scope of
the work, community profiles and adopted infrastructure standards.
Options for sanitation are compared on the basis of cost and
affordability with the cost estimates including capital, associated,
operational and discounted cost elements.

SANITATION OPTIONS/STORMWATER OPTIONS/
WATER SUPPLY/AQUA PRIVY

6216

LOW COST OPTIONS FOR URBAN SANITATION

URBAN EDGE VOL11 (10) 1987 p1-2

WORLD BANK
WASHINGTON DC

Provision of low-cost pour flush latrines in India on a large scale
is described as a replacement for scavengers and the bucket
system. Institutional approaches to provision of the system in
various States is discussed together with latrine costs.

POUR FLUSH LATRINES/BUCKET LATRINES/INDIA

SEE 1106
SEE 5107
SEE 5201

6301

WASTE MANAGEMENT IN URBAN SLUMS

AMOANING-YANKSON S.A.   1983

SANITATION AND WATER FOR DEVELOPMENT IN
AFRICA
9th WEDC CONFERENCE   HARARE   p50-53
LOUGHBOROUGH UNIVERSITY OF TECHNOLOGY

The Tema district council's attempts and trials at providing
sanitation are documented with details of an auto-flushing public
toilet together with costs and comments on its operation and
maintenance.

AUTO-FLUSH LATRINES/MAINTENANCE/GHANA

6302

URBAN LOW COST SANITATION

ASHWORTH J. de B.   1983

SANITATION AND WATER FOR DEVELOPMENT IN
AFRICA
9th WEDC CONFERENCE   HARARE   p93-95
LOUGHBOROUGH UNIVERSITY OF TECHNOLOGY

The choice between self, contractor or government built latrines is
reviewed with reference to the problems and advantages of each
method. A cost comparison of latrines built by each of the different
constructors is included.

COSTS/LATRINES/CONSTRUCTION MANAGEMENT

6303

GUIDE TO NEW SEWERAGE CONSTRUCTION

BS 8005 PART 1:1987   pp64

BRITISH STANDARDS INSTITUTION
MILTON KEYNES

The standard begins by detailing its scope and defining terms, materials and components within sewerage. Sections are included on design of surface water, foul sewers, combined sewers and manholes, as well as construction, testing and operation and maintenance.

SEWERS/SURFACE WATER/SEWERAGE/CONSTRUCTION/
OPERATION/MAINTENANCE

6304

MECHANISED EMPTYING OF PIT LATRINES IN AFRICA

CARROLL R.F.   1985

WATER AND SANITATION IN AFRICA
11th WEDC CONFERENCE   DAR ES SALAAM   p29-32
LOUGHBOROUGH UNIVERSITY OF TECHNOLOGY

Constraints on the types of system currently adopted for sludge removal are described and compared with the BREVAC suction tanker. Details are given on costs (to the householder), as well as operating and maintenance costs. The problems of site access are noted.

PIT EMPTYING/COSTS/OPERATION/MAINTENANCE/
VACUUM TRUCKS/ACCESS/BOTSWANA

6305

LOW COST LATRINE EMPTYING VEHICLE

COFFEY M.   1988 p77-80

WATER AND URBAN SERVICES IN ASIA AND THE
PACIFIC
14th WEDC CONFERENCE KUALA LUMPUR
LOUGHBOROUGH UNIVERSITY OF TECHNOLOGY

A description is given of tests carried out in lifting high density pit latrine sludges in Botswana as part of a project to develop a low-cost vehicle with a high capacity vacuum pump which could be manoeuvred into difficult areas, right up to the pit.

PIT LATRINES/PIT EMPTYING

6306

EMPTYING ON SITE EXCRETA DISPOSAL SYSTEMS
FIELD TESTS WITH MECHANISED EQUIPMENT IN

GABORONE BOTSWANA

IRCWD NEWS NO 21/22 1985   pp14

WHO INTERNATIONAL REFERENCE CENTRE FOR
WASTES DISPOSAL
DUEBENDORF

This summary of the field testing of a mechanised pit emptying service includes discussion of alternative techniques of pit emptying. Apart from the field tested equipment itself, alternatives examined included, Calabrese, Poole, Robla, and Brevac tankers, the ALH system and the Bumi hand pump.   The characteristics of the sludge are detailed.

PIT EMPTYING/SLUDGE/VACUUM TRUCKS/BOTSWANA

6307

EMPTYING ON SITE EXCRETA DISPOSAL SYSTEMS IN
DEVELOPING COUNTRIES: AN EVALUATION OF THE
PROBLEMS

IRCWD NEWS NO 17   1982 pp14

WHO INTERNATIONAL REFERENCE CENTRE FOR
WASTES DISPOSAL
DUEBENDORF

This review of current pit emptying technologies including vacuum trucks, outlines their emptying requirements in relation to the characteristics of the pit contents. A case study of emptying services in operation is outlined.

PIT EMPTYING/VACUUM TRUCKS/PIT LATRINES

6308

EXPERIENCES IN PLANNING AND IMPLEMENTING LOW
COST SANITATION

KSHIRSAGAR S.R.   1984

WATER AND SANITATION IN ASIA AND THE PACIFIC
10th WEDC CONFERENCE   SINGAPORE p184-187
LOUGHBOROUGH UNIVERSITY OF TECHNOLOGY

Factors contributing to the success of pour flush latrines in India are discussed including water availability, space and site condi-tions, construction materials, design, layout and pollution. The importance of administrative procedures, community participation and financing is also covered.

SANITATION/POLLUTION/COMMUNITY PARTICIPATION/
FINANCE/IMPLEMENTATION/INDIA

6309

STRATEGY FOR IMPLEMENTATION OF URBAN
SANITATION PROGRAMMES

NJAU F.Z.
BOYDELL R.A.   1982 16pp

IN: PROCEEDINGS OF A SEMINAR ON THE
IMPLEMENTATION OF LOW COST SANITATION
PROGRAMMES IN TANZANIA
ARUSHA CONFERENCE CENTRE
ARDHI INSTITUTE, MINISTRY OF LANDS, HOUSING AND
URBAN

An overview of sanitation options is given with definitions of the
problems of urban sanitation. Opportunities for cost recovery and
self help are discussed.

SANITATION OPTIONS/COST RECOVERY/
IMPLEMENTATION

6310

MANUAL ON DESIGN CONSTRUCTION AND
MAINTENANCE OF LOW COST POUR FLUSH
WATERSEAL LATRINES IN INDIA

ROY A.K.
CHATTERJEE P.K.
GUPTA K.N.
KHARE S.T.
RAU B.B.
SINGH R.S.   1984

TECHNOLOGY ADVISORY GROUP TECHNICAL NOTE 10
pp109
WORLD BANK
WASHINGTON DC

The manual covers construction, design, financing, institutional
involvement and operation and maintenance of pour flush latrines
in India. Also detailed are design distances from leach pits to
existing structures and water supplies etc. and the location of
drainage lines. Annexes contain working drawings, bills of
quantities, and cost summaries.

POUR FLUSH LATRINES/FINANCE/INDIA/COSTS/
OPERATION/MAINTENANCE

6311

IMPLEMENTATION PLAN FOR UNSEWERED AREAS -
DEMONSTRATION PROJECT IN GREATER CAIRO,
EGYPT

WARNER D.B.   1982   pp100

WASH FIELD REPORT NO 52

WATER AND SANITATION FOR HEALTH PROJECT
VIRGINIA

This implementation plan outlines the steps required to set up and
operate pilot demonstration projects for improved sanitation
methods. Methods for selecting suitable options are described
given objectives of minimising cost within the available time
schedule. Details of legal, constitutional, socio-cultural,
financial, technical and administrative constraints are included.
Possible methods for encouraging the adoption of improved
sanitation are discussed along with recommendations for the
solution of problems outlined.

SANITATION OPTIONS/EGYPT

6312

MINI TANKER DESIGNED TO SERVICE DENSE AREAS

URBAN EDGE VOL 11 (10) 1987 p5-6
WORLD BANK
WASHINGTON DC

Details are given of the design, cost and operation and
maintenance of a small prototype, low-cost vacuum tanker for
emptying pit latrines in dense squatter areas in Kenya.

PIT EMPTYING/VACUUM TANKER/COSTS/OPERATION/
MAINTENANCE/KENYA

6313

CONVERSION OF BUCKET PRIVIES INTO SANITARY
WATER-SEAL LATRINES

WHO SEMINAR 25-27 MAY 1978 pp51 + appendices

REGIONAL OFFICE FOR SOUTH EAST ASIA
WORLD HEALTH ORGANISATION
NEW DELHI

This review of efforts to eliminate bucket latrines in India
highlights the relationship between housing space and latrine
facilities. The government focus towards scavenger removal is
discussed within a wider appraisal of the Gujarat and Bihar
programmes. Topics covered in detail include government inputs,
costs and programme implementation, the extent of community
participation, and financial aspects of the programmes. An
analysis of the problems includes consideration of engineering
aspects, options for the unserved areas, and likely costs of
implementation.

BUCKET LATRINES/WATER SEAL LATRINES/
IMPLEMENTATION/INDIA/COMMUNITY PARTICIPATION/
OPTIONS/POUR FLUSH LATRINES

SEE 5301
SEE 5304

6401

QUETTA SEWERAGE AND DRAINAGE PROJECT
PAKISTAN

BKH CONSULTING ENGINEERS   1984

BKH CONSULTING ENGINEERS
THE HAGUE

The report describes a project which includes a proposal to provide
10,000 low-cost pour flush latrines in low-income areas. System
selection is made from options which include the pour flush,
vaults, communal facilities, septic tanks and sewers.   Costs of the
system.

POUR FLUSH LATRINES/VAULTS/COMMUNAL LATRINES/
SEPTIC TANKS/SEWERAGE/COSTS/PAKISTAN

6402

THE LATRINE PROJECT   MOZAMBIQUE

BRANDBERG B.   1985

IDRC MANUSCRIPT REPORT MR58e (Rev) pp 95
INTERNATIONAL DEVELOPMENT RESEARCH CENTRE
OTTAWA

This report documents the development of a number of different
types of latrines and the use of unreinforced domed concrete
cover slabs. Existing latrines and their components are described
and compared with the results of experiments on latrine designs,
construction techniques, management and training carried out in
Mozambique. Issues relating to project implementation and
institutional organisation are considered. Plans and details of
latrine types are also included.

LATRINES/MOZAMBIQUE

6403

PRIVATE CLEANLINESS AND PUBLIC SQUALOR

CHOWDHURY S.
SCHROEDER D.M.
WILLIAMS D.F.   1981

OXFAM SAIDPUR PILOT PROJECT INDIA pp84
OXFAM
OXFORD

Communal toilet facilities in Saidpur are described in the context
of a trial change from bucket latrines (with night soil collection) to
pour flush. The design, layout operation, maintenance and
financing arrangements of the Goalpara toilet block are detailed.

COMMUNAL LATRINES/OPERATION/MAINTENANCE/
FINANCE/BUCKET LATRINES/INDIA

6404

SANITATION IMPROVEMENTS IN INDONESIAN
KAMPUNGS

de KRUIJFF G.J.W.   1984

WATER AND SANITATION IN ASIA AND THE PACIFIC
10th WEDC CONFERENCE SINGAPORE   p176-179
LOUGHBOROUGH UNIVERSITY OF TECHNOLOGY

This overview of the Kampung Improvement Programme (KIP)
describes the existing water supply and sanitation facilities
including leach pits, desludging, communal sanitation facilities
and their operation and maintenance. Opportunities for semi-
private facilities and future programmes are also considered.

DESLUDGING/COMMUNUAL LATRINES/LEACH PITS/
OPERATION/MAINTENANCE/INDONESIA/WATER SUPPLY

6405

SANITATION FOR SITE AND SERVICES SCHEMES
KENYA: A TECHNICAL AND ECONOMIC APPRAISAL OF
SANITATION ALTERNATIVES FOR URBAN KENYA

de KRUIJFF G.J.W.   1980

HOUSING RESEARCH AND DEVELOPMENT UNIT   pp103
UNIVERSITY OF NAIROBI

This review of problems associated with waterborne sewerage in
Kenya compares conventional sewerage with alternatives such as
pour flush, aqua privy and VIP latrines. Constraints in Sites and
Services schemes and in their engineering aspects are discussed.
Also covered are principles of construction, design and pipe
material selection, as well as an economic costing and comparison
of the different sanitation technologies and options.

SANITATION OPTIONS/KENYA

6406

ASPECTS OF SANITATION FOR SITE AND SERVICE
SCHEMES - PAPER NO 6

de KRUIJFF G.J.W.   1980 pp6

IN: SEMINAR ON WATER SUPPLY AND DRAINAGE
SERVICES IN DEVELOPING COUNTRIES (S239)
NATIONAL BUILDING RESEARCH INSTITUTE
PRETORIA

The history of site and services in Kenya are outlined with
particular reference to sanitation in schemes in Kenya and the
development stages of serviced plots. Sanitation constraints and
options including sewered pour flush, sewered aqua privies and
VIP's are considered along with future developments.

VIP LATRINES/POUR FLUSH LATRINES/AQUA PRIVY/
KENYA

6407

PROCEEDINGS OF THE SEMINAR ON SEWAGE DISPOSAL
IN URBAN DEVELOPMENT (WITH PARTICULAR
REFERENCE TO LOW COST HOUSING)

DIVISION OF BUILDING RESEARCH
CSIRO 1971   pp67

CSIRO BOROKO
PAPUA NEW GUINEA

Waterborne sewerage systems in Papua New Guinea are described
and their advantages outlined in terms of health and convenience
over other sanitation systems. The use of septic tanks in urban
areas is discouraged.

SEWERAGE/SEPTIC TANKS/PAPUA NEW GUINEA

6408

ALTERNATIVE EXCRETA DISPOSAL SYSTEMS IN
EASTERN NIGERIA

EGBUNIWE N.   1980

WATER AND WASTE ENGINEERING IN AFRICA
6th WEDC CONFERENCE NIGERIA   p137-140
LOUGHBOROUGH UNIVERSITY OF TECHNOLOGY

This overview of sanitation in Eastern Nigeria as well as
describing the characteristics of faecal wastes includes a
discussion of existing technologies including open defecation, pier
latrines, pit latrines, bucket, septic tank and aqua privies.
Additional information includes tabulated summaries of the
features of disposal systems and maps of soil types in eastern
Nigeria.

PIT LATRINES/BUCKET LATRINES/SEPTIC TANKS/
AQUA PRIVY/PIER LATRINES/NIGERIA

6409

LOW COST SANITATION FOR KADUNA   NIGERIA

EKANEM E.J.   1988

Unpublished MSc thesis   pp128
LOUGHBOROUGH UNIVERSITY OF TECHNOLOGY

This project details the existing sanitary conditions as well as
water supply service levels in the low-income squatter and peri-
urban areas of Kaduna. Design and cost estimates are detailed for
low-cost sanitation systems which include VIP. ROEC, pour
flush, compost, aqua privy, septic tank. small bore sewers.

communal latrines, sullage, and solid waste disposal and
collection. Recommendations are included on implementation.

SANITATION OPTIONS/NIGERIA

6410

LOW COST SANITATION PROGRAMS IN INDIA

ENFO VOL 6 NO 1 1984   p10-11

ENVIRONMENTAL SANITATION INFORMATION CENTRE
ASIAN INSTITUTE OF TECHNOLOGY
BANGKOK

The change from bucket to pour flush latrines and communal
toilets is described along with the problems associated with the
introduction of Sulabh Shauchalaya's communal latrines.
Particular mention is made of the limited opportunity given for
installation by the community.

POUR FLUSH LATRINES/COMMUNUAL LATRINES

6411

SANITATION FOR LOW INCOME HOUSING JUBA SUDAN

FRANCEYS R.W.A   1987 14: 1-9

Preprint to
AFRICAN WATER TECHNOLOGY CONFERENCE NAIROBI
WORLD WATER
LIVERPOOL

The promotion of ventilated improved pit latrines for urban
sanitation is discussed. The need to match the costs with the
affordability and willingness to pay for a sanitation system is
emphasised, perhaps by means of normal consumer marketing.

VIP LATRINES/MARKETING/SUDAN

6412

LOW COST SANITATION ALTERNATIVES FOR PORT
HARCOURT   NIGERIA

GREEN S.I. 1987

Unpublished MSc thesis   pp107
LOUGHBOROUGH UNIVERSITY OF TECHNOLOGY

This review of the present methods of sanitation in Port Harcourt
and proposed low-cost sanitation alternatives includes sections on
water supply and sullage disposal (including design of facilities),
selection of sanitation systems (bucket, overhung, septic tank. pit
latrines, vaults, VIP, pour flush, and aqua privy), their
construction, design and operation and maintenance.

SANITATION OPTIONS/NIGERIA

6413

THE IMPROVEMNET OF DOMESTIC SANITATION IN
UNSEWERED AREAS OF KENYA

HOLLAND R.J.   1977

ENGINEERING FOR HEALTH IN HOT COUNTRIES
4th WEDC CONFERENCE   LOUGHBOROUGH p59-81
LOUGHBOROUGH UNIVERSITY OF TECHNOLOGY

Currently used disposal methods in Kenya (including bucket, pit,
septic tank, aqua privy, sewerage and cesspools) are summarised.
Comparisons between the systems are presented considering
technical and economic criteria (including unit cost) and
recommendations made regarding selection and improvement.

BUCKET LATRINES/PIT LATRINES/SEPTIC TANKS/
AQUA PRIVY/SEWERAGE/VAULTS/COSTS/KENYA

6414

UNIT COST OF DOMESTIC SEWAGE DISPOSAL IN KENYA

HOLLAND R.J.   1973

DEPARTMENT OF CIVIL ENGINEERING
UNIVERSITY OF NAIROBI

The costs of sewage disposal are analysed, including investment
and recurrent costs, for a range of systems used in Kenya including
bucket latrine, pit latrine, aqua privy, cesspit and piped sewerage.
The methods employed for each are also defined.

COSTS/BUCKET LATRINES/PIT LATRINES/AQUA PRIVY/
CESSPITS/SEWERAGE/KENYA

6415

SANITATION FOR LOW INCOME AREAS IN NYERI
KENYA

IRIMU J.M.   1988

Unpublished MSc thesis   pp143
LOUGHBOROUGH UNIVERSITY OF TECHNOLOGY

This project considers the different options for sanitation that are
feasible for low-income housing in Kenya. Background
information. The existing infrastructure. methods of sanitation and
levels of service are detailed. Design criteria, costs and
implementation problems of a range of alternatives options are
considered. which include pit latrines, VIP, ROEC, pour flush,
composting, cartage. public toilet. septic tanks and aqua privies.

KENYA/SANITATION OPTIONS/COSTS

6416

SANITATION SITE REPORT NO 1 IBADAN NIGERIA

IWUGO K.O.
MARA D.D.
FEACHEM R.G.   1978

APPROPRIATE TECHNOLOGY FOR WATER SUPPLY AND
WASTE
DISPOSAL IN DEVELOPING COUNTRIES
SANITATION STUDIES IN AFRICA   pp45
WORLD BANK
WASHINGTON DC

This report on existing sanitation facilities in Nigeria presents an
analysis of the economics and technical, and health considerations
related to pit, bucket and communal latrines.

PIT LATRINE/BUCKET LATRINES/COMMUNAL LATRINES/
COSTS/NIGERIA

6417

SANITATION SITE REPORT NO 2 NEW BUSSA NIGERIA

IWUGO K.O.
MARA D.D.
FEACHEM R.G.   1978

APPROPRIATE TECHNOLOGY FOR WATER SUPPLY AND
WASTE
DISPOSAL IN DEVELOPING COUNTRIES
SANITATION STUDIES IN AFRICA   pp24
WORLD BANK
WASHINGTON DC

Design and construction details and operation and maintenance
procedures for the New Bussa sewered aqua-privy system are
described. An economic analysis of sewered aqua-privies is
presented with both investment and recurrent costs considered.

AQUA PRIVY/COSTS/OPERATION/MAINTENANCE/
NIGERIA

6418

SANITATION SITE REPORT NO 3   KUMASI GHANA

IWUGO K.O.
MARA D.D.
FEACHEM R.G.   1978

APPROPRIATE TECHNOLOGY FOR WATER SUPPLY AND
WASTE
DISPOSAL IN DEVELOPING COUNTRIES
SANITATION STUDIES IN AFRICA   pp29
WORLD BANK
WASHINGTON DC

This site report includes a description of the existing facilities for sanitation, water supply, surface drainage, solid waste collection and disposal. The design and operation of the two most common sanitation methods, that is the bucket and aqua privy is detailed.

BUCKET LATRINES/AQUA PRIVY/WATER SUPPLY/
DRAINAGE/SOLID WASTE/GHANA

6419

SANITATION SITE REPORT NO 4 ZAMBIA

IWUGO K.O.
MARA D.D.
FEACHEM R.G.   1978

APPROPRIATE TECHNOLOGY FOR WATER SUPPLY AND
WASTE DISPOSAL IN DEVELOPING COUNTRIES
SANITATION STUDIES IN AFRICA   pp35
WORLD BANK
WASHINGTON DC

Sanitation facilities in the Zambian cities of Ndola and Lusaka are described. Sewerage in Lusaka including sewered aqua privy and pit latrines. Operation and maintenance experience of the sewered aqua privy, from both Lusaka and Ndola is discussed. Economic analysis of the Ndola sewerage and sanitation facilities includes consideration of investment and recurrent costs for both the aqua privy and pit latrine.

AQUA PRIVY/PIT LATRINE/COSTS/OPERATION/
MAINTENANCE/ZAMBIA

6420

SITE SELECTION FOR UPGRADING SANITATION IN LOW
INCOME NEIGHBOURHOODS IN TUNISIA

LALANDE F.
AYAD C.S.   1985

WASH FIELD REPORT NQ 143   pp152
WATER AND SANITATION FOR HEALTH PROJECT
VIRGINIA

The scope of the work was to determine the type of housing predominantly served by the existing infrastructure. Descriptions and details of improvements in sewerage and drainage are included together with reviews of costs and evaluations of construction plans for each site. Also presented is a methodology for site selection and analysis of socio-economic and engineering factors.

SEWERAGE/COSTS/TUNISIA

6421

ARDHI'S URBAN DEMONSTRATION PROJECT

MAKERERE D.J.   1982 pp18

IN: PROCEEDINGS OF A SEMINAR ON IMPLEMENTATION
OF LOW COST SANITATION PROGRAMMES IN
TANZANIA
ARUSHA INTERNATIONAL CONFERENCE CENTRE
ARDHI INSTITUTE AND MINISTRY OF LANDS, HOUSING
AND URBAN

A new design for the replacement of traditional pit latrines in low-income communities is described based on an adapted VIP taking into account religious and cultural attitudes.

VIP LATRINES/TANZANIA

6422

LOW COST SANITATION RESEARCH PROJECT
FINAL REPORT

MINISTRY OF LOCAL GOVERNMENT AND LANDS   1978
pp20 + appendix

MINISTRY OF LOCAL GOVERNMENT AND LANDS
GABORONE

The report describes a project undertaken to produce a sanitation system that had ease of operation and maintenance, low water use, was hygienic and culturally acceptable and of low-cost. Systems tested included compost, aqua privy and pit latrines and recommendations and experience with implementation are described.

COMPOST LATRINES/AQUA PRIVY/PIT LATRINE/BOTSWANA

6423

SANITARY WASTE DISPOSAL IN LOW INCOME
COMMUNITIES IN JAKARTA

MORROW D.   1975 pp77

Unpublished report
WORKSHOP II PUBLIC POLICY PROGRAMME
JAKARTA

Present conditions of waste disposal are described. Various options are reviewed within the low-income communities.

BUCKET LATRINES/VACUUM TRUCKS/AQUA PRIVIES/
INDONESIA

6424

LOW COST SANITATION IN INDIA; PROBLEMS AND
PROSPECTS

NATH K.J.
CHATTERJEE P.K   1984

WATER AND SANITATION IN ASIA AND THE PACIFIC
10th WEDC CONFERENCE   SINGAPORE   p188-191
LOUGHBOROUGH UNIVERSITY OF TECHNOLOGY

This paper reviews existing urban sanitation and examines
attempts at large scale provision of twin pour flush latrines in
urban areas. The status of bucket latrines is outlined and the
feasibility of twin pit pour flush discussed. Consideration is given
to technical and economic aspects, pollution risks and, legal and
institutional aspects.

POUR FLUSH LATRINES/BUCKET LATRINES/INDIA

6425

URBAN SANITATION SURVEY

NATIONAL HOUSING AUTHORITY   1979   pp94

NATIONAL HOUSING AUTHORITY
LUSAKA

This survey of sanitation facilities in Lusaka and Ndola, including
water and non-water borne, communal and bucket latrines
compared 7 existing systems. Conclusions of a social survey on
the appropriateness of individual systems are described and
recommendations made with reference to experimental systems in
Tanzania and Botswana.

W.C./AQUA PRIVY/PIT LATRINE/BUCKET LATRINES/
MAINTENANCE/COMMUNAL LATRINES/ZAMBIA

6426

IMMEDIATE PROGRAMME FOR SANITATION FOR
KAMPUNG IMPROVEMENT PROGRAMME OF JAKARTA

WHO PROJECT INO PIP-00Z (INS/72/068) 1977 pp250

NIHON SUIDO CONSULTANTS Co
TOKYO

Sanitation improvements in 88 Kampungs are detailed including
provision of public taps, waste disposal. surface drainage, sullage
disposal and solid waste.

PUBLIC TAPS/SURFACE DRAINAGE/SULLAGE/VAULTS/
COMMUNAL LATRINES/SOLID WASTE/INDONESIA

6427

SEWERAGE AND STORM DRAINAGE DESIGN FOR THE
CROSS RIVER HOUSING ESTATE CALABAR NIGERIA

NOAH J.I. 1986

Unpublished MSc thesis   pp154
WEDC DEPT OF CIVIL ENGINEERING
LOUGHBOROUGH UNIVERSITY OF TECHNOLOGY

Problems and solutions to the sewerage and drainage problems in
the study area are suggested after identification of the problems.
Attention is given to the design and operation and maintenance of
the systems.

STORM DRAINAGE/OPERATION/MAINTENANCE/NIGERIA

6428

LOW COST SANITATION IN NIGERIA

OLUWANDE P.A.
ONIBOKUN A.   1983

SANITATION AND WATER FOR DEVELOPMENT IN
AFRICA
9th WEDC CONFERENCE   HARARE   p54-58
LOUGHBOROUGH UNIVERSITY OF TECHNOLOGY

This brief statement of existing sanitation in Nigeria details a pilot
project undertaken to investigate both modified and conventional
latrines. Materials and methods are outlined and observations on
the project are discussed under headings which include self help,
socio economic, maintenance construction, costs and usage.

SANITATION OPTIONS/NIGERIA

6429

GRADUAL DEVELOPMENT OF SECTORAL SEWERAGE
PLAN

ORANGI PILOT PROJECT   CASE STUDY 1986 pp80

ORANGI PILOT PROJECT
KARACHI

Case studies of various areas in the Orangi pilot project are
presented with consideration of costs and technical problems in
both construction and maintenance.

SEWERAGE/MAINTENANCE/COSTS/PAKISTAN

6430

ORANGI PILOT PROJECT - THREE PROGRAMMES

ORANGI PILOT PROJECT   1984   pp19

ORANGI PILOT PROJECT
KARACHI

Details of existing low-cost sanitation is given together with the
problems with existing sanitation where sewerage discharges into
the lanes. The tasks involved in organising a low-cost sanitation
programme incorporating pour flush latrines and sewers are
outlined along with the per house cost.

POUR FLUSH LATRINES/SEWERAGE/PAKISTAN

6431

SANITATION FOR BALDIA TOWNSHIP   KARACHI

PICKFORD J.A.
REED R.   1979   pp46

Unpublished report
WATER ENGINEERING AND DEVELOPMENT CENTRE
LOUGHBOROUGH UNIVERSITY OF TECHNOLOGY

This report on the existing sanitation facilities in Baldia with a
review of alternatives, includes design and construction
recommendations for pour flush latrines. Tables present data on
the water supply, soil survey, and a survey of the condition of
existing pit latrines.

POUR FLUSH LATRINES/SULLAGE/SOLID WASTE/
STORM DRAINAGE/PAKISTAN

6432

LOW COST WATER SEAL LATRINE PROGRAMME IN
URBAN COMMUNITIES OF INDIA

ROY A.K.
GUPTA K.N.
RAU B.B.
RAJ DEV
BHASKARAN T.R.   1980 pp35

INTERNATIONAL SEMINAR ON LOW COST
TECHNOLOGIES FOR   THE DISPOSAL OF HUMAN
WASTES IN URBAN COMMUNITIES CALCUTTA
TECHNOLOGY ADVISORY GROUP FOR INDIA 1980
UNDP GLOBAL PROJECT GLO/78/006

The report introduces the development of urban sanitation in this
area in India, with analysis of the problems, customs, attitudes,
technical and financial aspects. Details of the scope of the project
are given together with costs and bill of quantities for the pour
flush   latrine and for the conversion from dry to pour flush

systems. Working drawings and details of the system are
appended.

POUR FLUSH LATRINES/COSTS/INDIA

6433

APPLICABILITY OF SMALL BORE GRAVITY SEWERS IN
ADDIS ABABA

SAHLE H.   1988   pp47

Unpublished MSc thesis
INSTITUTE OF WATER AND ENVIRONMENTAL
ENGINEERING
TAMPERE UNIVERSITY OF TECHNOLOGY

The thesis examines the characteristics of domestic waste water
and considers the role of small bore systems including components
and principles. The technical advantages and disadvantages are
described along with planning, design of the   system (including
interceptor tank), and operation and maintenance. Municipal
wastewater disposal practices in Addis Ababa are related to the
costs of a designed example of the proposed system.

SMALL BORE SEWERS/INTERCEPTOR TANKS/
WASTEWATER/COSTS/ETHIOPIA

6434

EIGHT CASE STUDIES OF RURAL AND URBAN FRINGE
AREAS IN LATIN AMERICA

SALINAS B.
CACERES R.   1979

REPORT PU RES 23   pp230
WORLD BANK
WASHINGTON DC

Eight case studies are described to provide planners with an
understanding of human behaviour patterns which affect factors
such as acceptability and maintenance of water and sanitation
systems. An economic analysis is included.

PIT LATRINES/POUR FLUSH LATRINES/GUATEMALA/
MEXICO/SAN SALVADOR/COLUMBIA/NICARAGUA/HAITI

6435

SCAVENGING FREE SCHEME FOR VRINDAVAN

SULABH SHAUCHALAYA 1986 pp51

SULABH INTERNATIONAL
NEW DELHI

The report details a project to convert all the bucket latrines to
pour flush types with a description of the existing sanitation

facilities. Project proposals are outlined covering construction and householder involvement, operation and maintenance, and finance. Cost estimates for conversion to pour flush are also detailed.

POUR FLUSH LATRINES/OPERATION/MAINTENANCE/
FINANCE/COSTS/INDIA

6436

THIRD WORLD SANITATION OPTIONS
THE ZAMBIAN CASE

TODD D.M.   1985

ENVIRONMENTALIST VOL 5 (2)   p111-121

Detailed strategies for the provision of sanitation in Zambia's low-income housing areas are outlined supported by performance data for a range of options including W.C's connected to sewers or septic tanks, aqua privies connected to soakaways or septic tanks, and communal W.C's. Alternative systems evaluated include pit latrines, pour flush and vaults.

SEWERAGE/VAULTS/SEPTIC TANKS/
COMMUNAL LATRINES/POUR FLUSH LATRINES/
SOAKAWAYS/ZAMBIA

6437

SEPTIC TANK SYSTEMS IN URBAN SABAH

WANG. B.C.C.   1982   pp66

Unpublished MSc thesis
LOUGHBOROUGH UNIVERSITY OF TECHNOLOGY

This review of septic tank systems and their use in an urban environment considers issues of public health, and performance and the advantages of soakaways.   Cost comparisons are presented with other regions along with design recommendations covering such aspects as plot sizes.

SEPTIC TANK/SOAKAWAYS/COSTS/PLOT SIZES/
MALAYSIA

6438

THE IMPLEMENTATION OF URBAN AND RURAL
SANITATION PROGRAMMES IN BOTSWANA

WILSON J.G.   1983

SANITATION AND WATER FOR DEVELOPMENT IN
AFRICA
9th WEDC CONFERENCE   HARARE   p46-49
LOUGHBOROUGH UNIVERSITY OF TECHNOLOGY

This paper concentrates on the existing and proposed methodologies, costing and experiences from Botswana urban

sanitation programmes. Issues covered include user attitudes to REC II [Revised Earth Closet], construction monitoring and improvements, cost reductions and contractor imputs.

BOTSWANA/REC II/COSTS

SEE 1406
SEE 1410
SEE 1414
SEE 1412
SEE 1420
SEE 1421
SEE 1426
SEE 5103
SEE 5206
SEE 5405

Section 7. SOLID WASTE

7101

SOLID WASTE MANAGEMENT

ATTATWALA F.A.   1986   pp98

ALL INDIA INSTITUTE OF LOCAL SELF-GOVERNMENT
BOMBAY

This review of solid waste systems includes descriptions of waste
composition, storage disposal and collection methods. Public street
cleansing and transportation systems are described (with drawings
of equipment) together with their management, organisation and
financial control in an Indian context. Data presented includes
tables on garbage analysis, waste classification, rate of production
of wastes from various sources, and collection systems.

SOLID WASTE/SOLID WASTE COLLECTION/
STREET CLEANSING/SOLID WASTE MANAGEMENT/
FINANCE/INDIA

7102

RECYCLING OF SOLID WASTES

ENVIRONMENTAL SANITATION REVIEWS No 13/14 1984
pp140

ENVIRONMENTAL SANITATION INFORMATION CENTRE
ASIAN INSTITUTE OF TECHNOLOGY
BANGKOK

This introduction to recycling includes discussion of the
appropriateness of recycling in developing countries, the
characteristics of solid waste and application of reuse. Materials
considered for recycling include paper, glass, plastics and
metals and options for energy recovery, composting as well as
socio-economic considerations.

RECYCLING/SOLID WASTE COLLECTION

7103

RECYCLING POTENTIALS OF SOLID WASTE IN ASIA
THROUGH ORGANISED SCAVENGING

LOHANI B.N.   1984

CONSERVATION AND RECYCLING VOL7 (2-4)   p181-190
PERGAMON PRESS
OXFORD

This review of solid waste and technically appropriate solutions
in Asia examines recycling options with regard to socio-
economic status. The Asian context is examined with sections on

waste in Asia, climate, financial restraints, social and religious
constraints. Technical options for resource recovery are
discussed including composting, scavenging and recycling
through sorting, collection and organised scavenging.

SOLID WASTE COLLECTION/FINANCE/RECYCLING

7104

URBAN SOLID WASTE

NATH K.J.
CHATTERJEE, P.K.
DASGUPTA, S.K.
DE, D.M. 1983

SANITATION AND WATER FOR DEVELOPMENT IN
AFRICA
9TH WEDC CONFERENCE   HARARE p31-34
LOUGHBOROUGH UNIVERSITY OF TECHNOLOGY

The existing status of solid waste in small and medium towns in
India is described along with details of pilot studies. Alternative
disposal methods and waste materials are described in relation to
their collection, transportation and disposal.

SOLID WASTE DISPOSAL/COSTS/INDIA

7105

COMPOSTING OF DOMESTIC REFUSE

RABBANI K.R.
JINDAL R.
KUBOTA H.   1983

ENVIRONMENTAL SANITATION REVIEWS No 10/11
pp107
ENVIRONMENTAL SANITATION INFORMATION CENTRE
ASIAN INSTITUTE OF TECHNOLOGY
BANGKOK

The problems of disposal, and the principals and fundamentals of
composting are discussed here with reference to environmental
factors and kinetics, and technological aspects. Topics covered
include compost maturity, final processes and handling and
relevant public health and economic aspects with a case study
illustration.

SOLID WASTE DISPOSAL/ECONOMICS/COMPOSTING

7106

SOLID WASTE MANAGEMENT

7106

SOLID WASTE MANAGEMENT
SELECTED TOPICS

SUESS M.J. (ED)   1985   pp210

WORLD HEALTH ORGANISATION
REGIONAL OFFICE EUROPE
COPENHAGEN

This review of land disposal includes such aspects as planning
the site, site survey, preparatory work, acceptable wastes,
operational practice, land restoration, economic considerations
and the opportunities for composting, incineration, and handling
animal wastes.

SOLID WASTE DISPOSAL/ECONOMICS

SEE 1103
SEE 1104
SEE 1105
SEE 1108
SEE 1109
SEE 1110
SEE 1111
SEE 1423
SEE 1112
SEE 1113
SEE 5107

7201

SOLID WASTE MANAGEMENT: REDUCING COSTS

URBAN EDGE   VOL 11 No 6 1987

WORLD BANK
WASHINGTON DC

The article explores the opportunities for reducing the costs of
solid waste management by selecting appropriate equipment,
reducing travel time, improving routing,   preventative
maintenance and   community participation. A table
summarising municipal waste sources.

SOLID WASTE MANAGEMENT/MAINTENANCE/
COMMUNITY PARTICIPATION/COSTS

SEE 1204
SEE 1209
SEE 1230
SEE 1233
SEE 6208

7301

SOLID WASTE MANAGEMENT IN DEVELOPING
COUNTRIES

BHIDE A. D.
SUNDARESAN B.B.   1982

INSDOC REPORT No 2 pp222
INDIAN SCIENTIFIC DOCUMENTATION CENTRE
NEW DELHI

This review of solid waste management sets out the typical
quantities and characteristics of solid waste, including industrial
and hazardous waste. Waste management is described under the
following headings of collection, equipment, composting, land
disposal and incineration, with consideration of future processing
methods, and legislative implications for disposal.

SOLID WASTE MANAGEMENT/VEHICLES/COMPOSTING

7302

DECENTRALISED SOLID WASTE COLLECTION
FACILITIES

CLARK R.M.
HELMS W.P.   1970

JOURNAL OF THE SANITARY ENGINEERING DIVISION
ASCE VOL96 SA5   p1035-1043
AMERICAN SOCIETY OF CIVIL ENGINEERS

The paper presents an alternative collection model with likely
operating costs and an example problem and solution.

SOLID WASTE COLLECTION/COSTS

7303

INTERCOUNTRY WORKSHOP ON SOLID WASTE
MANAGEMENT; DAMASCUS

COAD A.   1983

WORLD HEALTH ORGANISATION
ALEXANDRIA

The report describes a workshop with topic areas on the sources
and characteristics of solid waste (including street refuse), aspects
of its storage and collection and socio-economic and health
aspects. Waste management including treatment and disposal is
discussed comparing options of landfill, composting and resource
recovery. The influence of institutions and legislation is also
considered.

SOLID WASTE MANAGEMENT/LANDFILL

7304

ENVIRONMENTAL MANAGEMENT OF URBAN SOLID
WASTES IN DEVELOPING COUNTRIES : A PROJECT
GUIDE

COINTREAU S.   1982 pp214

TECHNICAL PAPER No 5
WORLD BANK URBAN DEVELOPMENT DEPARTMENT
WORLD BANK
WASHINGTON DC

This paper as well as defining the characteristics and generation
rates of urban waste, discusses management issues and problems in
relation to waste delivery (including collection, transfer and
disposal) and solid waste improvement programmes. Institutional
arrangements and costs are also considered.

SOLID WASTE MANAGEMENT/COSTS/
SOLID WASTE COLLECTION/SOLID WASTE DISPOSAL

7305

MANAGEMENT OF SOLID WASTES IN DEVELOPING
COUNTRIES

FLINTOFF F.   1976

WHO REGIONAL PUBLICATION
SOUTH EAST ASIA SERIES No 1   pp244
WORLD HEALTH ORGANISATION
NEW DELHI

Methods of sampling, storing and collecting waste are described
and the influence of factors such as the frequency of collection,
type of collection vehicles and nature of the collection points
discussed. Treatment and disposal options are outlined including,
sanitary landfill and composting, together with a consideration of
the economies of refuse collection.

SOLID WASTE COLLECTION/VEHICLES/
SOLID WASTE DISPOSAL/LANDFILL/STREET CLEANSING

7306

PUBLIC CLEANSING

FLINTOFF F.
MILLARD R.   1969   pp475

MACLAREN AND SONS
LONDON

Refuse definitions are presented based on yield and analysis, and
methods suggested for storage in both small and large buildings.
Methods of collection and disposal are compared including on site
disposal, collection vehicles, the merits of transfer stations, land
reclamation and street   cleansing.

SOLID WASTE STORAGE/SOLID WASTE COLLECTION/
SOLID WASTE DISPOSAL/VEHICLES/
TRANSFER STATIONS/STREET CLEANSING

7307

MANAGING SOLID WASTES IN DEVELOPING COUNTRIES

HOLMES J.R. (ed) 1984   pp304

JOHN WILEY AND SONS
CHICHESTER

Solid waste management decisions in developing countries are
explored using studies in countries which include India, Africa,
Iran and Indonesia. Collection practice, problems and planning,
together with trends in solid waste management in developing
countries are discussed.

SOLID WASTE MANAGEMENT/INDIA/AFRICA/IRAN/
INDONESIA

7308

URBAN SOLID WASTE: APPROPRIATE TECHNOLOGY

NATH K.J.
CHATTERJEE P.K.
DASGUPTA S.K.
DE D.M. 1983

SANITATION AND WATER FOR DEVELOPMENT IN
AFRICA
9TH WEDC CONFERENCE   HARARE p31-34
LOUGHBOROUGH UNIVERSITY OF TECHNOLOGY

Analysis of solid waste management in India is presented based
on a survey of 34 municipal towns, and compared with data from
a pilot study using alternative methods. The operation and
maintenance costs of the study are tabulated.

SOLID WASTE MANAGEMENT/INDIA/OPERATION/COSTS

7309

MATCHING SOLID WASTE COLLECTION TO LOCAL
CAPABILITY

OUANO E.A.R
PESCOD M.B.   p82-102

SOLID WASTE MANAGEMENT IN SOUTH EAST ASIA
REGIONAL SEMINAR   THAILAND 1975
WHO REGIONAL OFFICE FOR SOUTH EAST ASIA
NEW DELHI

This review of aspects of waste collection in Thailand,
provides details of the ground condition, and waste collection

process, and analysis of the system. Characteristics of the area, together with a cost analysis are also included.

SOLID WASTE COLLECTION/THAILAND/COSTS

7310

STORAGE AND PRIMARY COLLECTION OF URBAN SOLID WASTE

THAKUR B.B.
DEY D.N.
NATH K.J.   1986

WATER AND SANITATION AT MID DECADE
12th WEDC CONFERENCE   CALCUTTA   p112-115
LOUGHBOROUGH UNIVERSITY OF TECHNOLOGY

This overview of solid waste management in Calcutta, identifies the deficiencies in the present system and outlines a proposed new system which includes house to house collection, transfer stations, composting and sanitary landfill. Primary collection vehicles include hand, animal carts and tricycles.

SOLID WASTE COLLECTION/LANDFILL/INDIA

7311

REFUSE COLLECTION VEHICLES FOR DEVELOPING COUNTRIES

UNCHS HS/138/88/E 1988   pp53

UNITED NATIONS CENTRE FOR HUMAN SETTLEMENTS
NAIROBI

General principles of solid waste management, and system optimisation, are discussed as they are influenced by collection costs, appraisal and charges. Emphasis is given to considering the factors affecting selection of the waste collection system and choice of refuse collection vehicles.

SOLID WASTE MANAGEMENT/
REFUSE COLLECTION VEHICLES/COSTS/TARIFFS

7401

SOLID WASTE MANAGEMENT IN BENIN CITY   NIGERIA

AGBONIFO S.A.O.   1982 pp65

Unpublished MSc thesis
LOUGHBOROUGH UNIVERSITY OF TECHNOLOGY

This project details methods of collection and disposal of solid waste in Benin City as well as discussing problems of management. Typical waste generation rates are analysed and costs presented for a model design of a transfer station.

SOLID WASTE COLLECTION/SOLID WASTE DISPOSAL/
COSTS/NIGERIA

7402

A CASE STUDY IN SOLID WASTE GENERATION AND CHARACTERISTICS IN IRAN

COAD M.A.   p91-102

IN: MANAGING SOLID WASTES IN DEVELOPING COUNTRIES
HOLMES J.R. (ED)
JOHN WILEY AND SONS 1984
CHICHESTER

Data on the composition and weight per capita of solid waste for various social groups in the city of Shiraz, Iran are presented. Recommendations are made regarding improvements to collection and transfer of solid waste.

SOLID WASTE MANAGEMENT/IRAN

7403

PRELIMINARY REPORT ON SOLID WASTE MANAGEMENT IN COLOMBO   SRI LANKA

COINTREAU S.J.
CUMMINGS R.
CERRATO D.
ARMSTRONG W.
BERGER A.   1981

COLOMBO MUNICIPAL COUNCIL
COLOMBO

Aspects of the study area described include institutional and financial arrangements, waste collection, disposal, recycling and management costs. Conclusions and recommendations regarding waste management are included.

SOLID WASTE MANAGEMENT/FINANCE/RECYCLING/
SRI LANKA

7404

SOLID WASTE MANAGEMENT:
THE PHILIPPINE EXPERIENCE

GADI M.T. 1984

WATER AND SANITATION IN ASIA AND THE PACIFIC
10th WEDC CONFERENCE   SINGAPORE   p155-158
LOUGHBOROUGH UNIVERSITY OF TECHNOLOGY

This review of solid waste systems in the Philippines, as well as describing the present state of solid waste management examines the efforts being made to implement improvements. Topics covered include waste storage, sources, collection, transportation, recycling, and disposal, with consideration of the options for financial support.

SOLID WASTE MANAGEMENT/PHILIPPINES

7405

IMPROVEMENT OF A SOLID WASTE COLLECTION SYSTEM   A CASE OF GIVATAYIM ISRAEL

RONEN R.
KELLARMAN A.
LAPIDOT M.   1983

APPLIED GEOGRAPHY 3 (2)   p133-144
BUTTERWORTH
LONDON

Several models for optimum routing solid waste are examined for the Givatauym case study area in an attempt to derive solutions to the expensive collection methods currently used. Consideration is given to alternative collection systems, quantities, budgets, and routing.

SOLID WASTE COLLECTION/ISRAEL

7406

SOLID WASTE MANAGEMENT IN A LARGE SQUATTER SETTLEMENT IN KARACHI

SINNATAMBY G.N. 1986

IN: UNCHS SEMINAR ON CITY CLEANSING WITHIN THE FRAMEWORK OF ENVIRONMENTAL PROTECTION, CAIRO 1986, pp22

UNITED NATIONS CENTRE FOR HUMAN SETTLEMENTS NAIROBI

The report considers settlement characteristics and composition of the refuse and options for storage and collection facilities on the basis of cost and affordability. Methods of treatment are discussed including composting and recommendations on collection systems made.

SOLID WASTE MANAGEMENT/GENERATION/STORAGE/
COSTS/AFFORDABILITY/PAKISTAN

7407

STUDY OF THE CHARACTERISTICS AND QUANTITY OF SOLID WASTES IN LAHORE

TARIQ K. 1981

REPORT 048-4-81

INSTITUTE OF PUBLIC HEALTH ENGINEERING
UNIVERSITY OF ENGINEERING AND TECHNOLOGY,
LAHORE

The study presents data on the characteristics and quantity of solid waste generation in Lahore. The data is analysed according to the different zones of the Lahore Municipal Council.

SOLID WASTE QUANTITY/SOLID WASTE COMPOSITION/
PAKISTAN

7408

SOLID WASTE: THE GARBAGE WAR: NEED FOR DEFENCE

URBAN EDGE   VOL 3   NO 8   1979   pp1-6

WORLD BANK
WASHINGTON DC

Strategies for improved garbage collection in Calcutta, Jakarta and   Manila are described including examples of recycling in Columbia   and   Egypt and the encouragement of scavengers. The issue of landfill versus composting and the implications of industrial pollution are discussed.

SOLID WASTE COLLECTION/LANDFILL/RECYCLING/
INDIA/INDONESIA/PHILIPPINES/COLUMBIA/EGYPT

7409

URBAN SOLID WASTE MANAGEMENT IN TANZANIA

YHDEGO M. 1988

WASTE MANAGEMENT AND RESEARCH VOL 6(2) 175-194
INTERNATIONAL SOLID WASTE AND PUBLIC
CLEANSING ASSOCIATION
LONDON

The background to solid waste disposal in Tanzania is discussed outlining the quantities of waste generated and its composition. Options for collection, transportation, on-site staorage and disposal are considered together with their administration and management requirements.

SOLID WASTE MANAGEMENT/TANZANIA

SEE 1236
SEE 1406
SEE 1407
SEE 1410
SEE 1420
SEE 1427
SEE 1415
SEE 1431
SEE 5407
SEE 6431
SEE 6426

Section 8. POWER

8101

ELECTRICITY SUPPLY

ANGLO AMERICAN COUNCIL ON PRODUCTIVITY   1949
pp129

ANGLO AMERICAN COUNCIL ON PRODUCTIVITY
NEW YORK \ LONDON

The section on distribution deals with the engineering aspects of
urban and rural distribution system planning   and design with a
comparison between US and UK practice.   Detail is given on
system planning (aspects of sub stations, transformers and
maintenance), urban distribution (including overhead cables and
underground distribution), rural distribution (including pole
transformers) and meter practice.

ELECTRICAL DISTRIBUTION/TRANSFORMERS/
MAINTENANCE/CABLES

8102

DESIGN OF LOW VOLTAGE DISTRIBUTION NETWORKS

CARSON M.J.
CORNFIELD G.   1973

PROCEEDINGS OF THE INSTITUTION OF ELECTRICAL
ENGINEERS VOL 120   p585-592
LONDON

A computer based method for low voltage network design is
described together with design procedures and detail of the theory
of the cost function including selection and design of the network.

ELECTRICAL DISTRIBUTION/COSTS

8103

TRANSMISSION AND DISTRIBUTION OF ELECTRICAL
ENERGY

COTTON H.
BARBER H.   1970   3rd edition pp472

THE ENGLISH UNIVERSITY PRESS
LONDON

This summary of power systems analysis includes consideration of
economics as well as technical design and construction of
distributors, overhead lines including conductors   and supports,
insulated cables including low voltage cables and circuit breakers.

OVERHEAD LINES/ELECTRICAL DISTRIBUTION

8104

OVERHEAD LINE PRACTICE

COX E.H.   1975

PROCEEDINGS OF THE INSTITUTION OF ELECTRICAL
ENGINEERS VOL 122   p1009-1017
LONDON

This British Electrical Board specification covers: conductors,
joints, medium voltage lines, high voltage lines on wooden
poles, overhead line insulators, high voltage line tapping, wood
pole preservation, (decay and treatment) and concrete poles.

POWER POLES/OVERHEAD LINES

8105

SOLAR PHOTOVOLTAIC PRODUCTS
A GUIDE TO DEVELOPMENT WORKERS

DERRICK A.
FRANCIS C.
BOKALDERS V.   1989   pp127

INTERMEDIATE TECHNOLOGY PUBLICATIONS
LONDON

This overview of photovoltaics includes sections on history,
processes and systems, implementation, battery technology and
applications such as water pumping, refrigeration, and lighting
among others.

PHOTOVOLTAIC ELECTRICITY/LIGHTING/SOLAR POWER

8106

A COURSE IN TRANSMISSION AND DISTRIBUTION

DHIR S.M.
GARG G.C
GIRDHAR S.K.   1977   pp186

SATYA PRAKASHAN
NEW DELHI

The publication includes sections on, distribution (low tension
feeders and distributors), low and high tension underground and
overhead cables, and sub stations (including pole mounted
transformers).

ELECTRICAL DISTRIBUTION/CABLES/TRANSFORMERS

8107

INVESTIGATION INTO STANDARDS OF URBAN
ELECTRICITY DISTRIBUTION

ELECTRICITY COUNCIL UK 1973   pp33 + appendix

BOLEY, T.A.
BROWN, G.H.
PRIOR, F.H.

WORLD BANK
WASHINGTON DC

This review of design practice in developing countries includes an evaluation of systems design, as related to estimation of load and choice of system. The social and economic consequences of varying the quality of service are considered.

ELECTRICAL DISTRIBUTION/ECONOMICS

8108

IEE WIRING REGULATIONS FOR ELECTRICAL INSTALLATIONS 15th EDITION

INSTITUTION OF ELECTRICAL ENGINEERS 1981 pp220

INSTITUTION OF ELECTRICAL ENGINEERS
LONDON

The scope, objectives and requirements of the standards relate to safe practice. Recommendations cover the selection and erection of equipment, inspection and testing and safety procedures.

ELECTRICAL STANDARDS/WIRING

8109

ROAD LIGHTING IN DEVELOPING COUNTRIES

INSTITUTION OF LIGHTING ENGINEERS 1990 pp36

INSTITUTION OF LIGHTING ENGINEERS
RUGBY

A useful introduction to the subject of street lighting with good diagrams. UK practise adapted for use in developing countries.

STREET LIGHTING

8110

IES LIGHTING HANDBOOK APPLICATIONS VOLUME

KAUFMAN J.E.
HAYNES H.   1981

ILLUMINATING ENGINEERING SOCIETY OF NORTH AMERICA
NEW YORK

This handbook details design criteria and methods for residential

and road lighting with definitions of the types of systems and standard classification.

STREET LIGHTING

8111

UNDERGROUND POWER CABLES

KING S.Y.
HALFTER N.A.   1982   pp411

LONGMANS
LONDON

This overview of power cables describes power cables and their components including materials, screening, types of underground cable, and the use of cables for low voltage distribution as well as giving guidance on cable design.

UNDERGROUND CABLES

8112

ELECTRICITY DISTRIBUTION NETWORK DESIGN: IEE POWER ENGINEERING SERIES 9.

LAKERVI E.
HOLMES E.J.   1989 pp320

PEREGRINUS
INSTITUTION OF ELECTRICAL ENGINEERS
LONDON

This detailed technical guide to the planning of distribution networks, considers high, medium and low voltage systems. Consideration is given to equipment selection, system protection, substations, loads, special loads and network voltage performance along with computer-aided network design.

ELECTRICAL DISTRIBUTION/ECONOMICS/POWER LOADS

8113

PLANNING OF DISTRIBUTION SYSTEMS IN DEVELOPING COUNTRIES

MENON S.G.
RAO B.   B.V.R. 1986

PROCEEDINGS OF THE INSTITUTION OF ELECTRICAL ENGINEERS VOL 133 PART C NO 7 p384-388
LONDON

Planning issues considered include load forecasting and estimating for domestic, commercial, public institutions and industrial consumers. An economic analysis presents tabulated data on consumption levels as related to income, commercial loads, public institutions, street lighting and demand patterns.

ELECTRICAL DISTRIBUTION/STREET LIGHTING

8114

SOLAR POWER ELECTRICITY
A SURVEY OF PHOTOVOLTAIC POWER IN DEVELOPING
COUNTRIES

McNELIS B.
DERRICK A.
STARR M.   1988   pp87

UNESCO/INTERMEDIATE TECHNOLOGY PUBLICATIONS
LONDON

Specific applications of solar power in developing countries is
described with detail on water pumping, refrigeration, lighting and
the opportunities for rural electrification among other applications.

PHOTOVOLTAIC ELECTRICITY/LIGHTING/SOLAR POWER

8115

LOW VOLTAGE DISTRIBUTION BY PVC INSULATED SWA
CABLE

SAULEZ K.J.   1967   p237-247

ELECTRICAL RESEARCH ASSOCIATION DISTRIBUTION
CONFERENCE PART 1 3-6 18.67
EDINBURGH

The report describes an assessment of the relative cost of overhead
systems and underground PVC SWA systems for medium sized
sites in Uganda. Costs were found to be roughly comparable with
considerable advantages of appearance, safety and maintenance for
the underground cables.

ELECTRICAL DISTRIBUTION/UNDERGROUND CABLES/
UGANDA

8116

A SURVEY OF STREET LIGHTING AND ITS FUTURE

STEVENS W.R.
FERGUSON H.M.   1961

PROCEEDINGS OF THE INSTITUTION OF ELECTRICAL
ENGINEERS VOL 108   p127-135
LONDON

The principles of street lighting are discussed with reference to
U.K. street lighting practice. Topics considered include space to
height ratios, costs, the use of side street lights and trends in
street lighting abroad using a lighting case study.

STREET LIGHTING/COSTS

8117

ELECTRIC POWER DISTRIBUTION

TAYLOR E.O.
BOAL G.A. et al 1966 pp272

EDWARD ARNOLD PUBLISHERS
LONDON

The design of minimum cost urban power distribution networks is
considered including urban load, and specification of cables and
substations. The economic constraints of distribution in developing
countries is discussed as part as an overall strategy of rural
development.

ELECTRICAL DISTRIBUTION/COSTS/CABLES/
SUB-STATIONS

8118

STREET LIGHTING

WALDRAM J.M. 1952 pp431

EDWARD ARNOLD
LONDON

This comprehensive text addresses the fundamental principles of
street lighting with consideration of such aspects as the distribution
of light, light height, spacing and power requirements, the needs
of different road surfaces, network layouts and installation as well
as equipment requirements and costs. Other issues discussed
include distribution options, (including underground and overhead
cables), photoelectric control, maintenance requirements and
continental and U.S.practice, specifications and codes.

STREET LIGHTING/COSTS/MAINTENANCE

8119

ROAD LIGHTING DESIGN

WRIGHT P.D.   1988

MUNICIPAL ENGINEER VOL 5 (1) p25-34
THOMAS TELFORD
LONDON

This summary of the British standard code of practice, discusses
design and quality criteria for road lighting, requirements for good
vision and outlines road lighting principles.

STREET LIGHTING

8120

DESIGN HANDBOOK FOR PHOTOVOLTAIC POWER
SYSTEMS

YOUNG S.K. 1981

SANDIA NATIONAL LABS
ALBUQUERQUE

This handbook describes simplified analysis methodologies for the
design of on-site (5 kW to 500 kW) and utility connected
photovoltaic power systems. Included is consideration of energy
loads, system sizing and design details as well as an economic
comparison with conventional systems.

PHOTOVOLTAIC ELECTRICITY

SEE 1103
SEE 1104
SEE 1105
SEE 1107
SEE 1108
SEE 1109
SEE 1110
SEE 1111
SEE 1233

8201

THE ECONOMICS OF LOW VOLTAGE ELECTRICITY
SUPPLY TO NEW HOUSING ESTATES

COPLAND F.G.   1952

PROCEEDINGS OF THE INSTITUTION OF ELECTRICAL
ENGINEERS VOL 99 (118) Part 1   p95-106
LONDON

The report considers the economics of design in relation to
theoretical distribution networks, and alternative methods of
voltage regulation and includes data on typical power demands and
losses. Alternative system costs are tablulated.

ELECTRICITY DEMAND/ECONOMICS/COST

SEE 1204
SEE 1106

8301

OVERHEAD LINE PRACTICE

McCOMBE J.   1955   pp287

MACDONALD
LONDON

The report details recommendations on setting out of overhead
lines, foundations for poles, methods of preservation and testing
for wood poles, support and cross arm design, and design and
installation of stays, insulators, conductors and pole mounted
transformers.

POWER POLES/SUB STATIONS/OVERHEAD LINES

8302

DISTRIBUTION AND MAINTENANCE OF ELECTRIC
SUPPLY   AND PUBLIC HEALTH ENGINEERING SERVICES
IN CANTONMENTS AND TOWNSHIPS

NADGIR K.N.
MURTHY C.K.
SHETTY M.S.
MURTHY C.R.N.
MURTHY K.R. 1973

PROCEEDINGS OF A SEMINAR AT THE COLLEGE OF
MILITARY ENGINEERING   pp439
THE INSTITUTION OF MILITARY ENGINEERS
PUNE

ELECTRICAL DISTRIBUTION

8401

STANDARDS OF URBAN ELECTRICITY DISTRIBUTION
C.F.E. MEXICO - CASE STUDY

ELECTRICITY COUNCIL UK.

BROWN G.H.
BOLEY T.A   1973   pp48 + appendices

FOR WORLD BANK
WASHINGTON DC

This review of C.F.E. included an examination of their investment
programme, the reliability of supply and the criteria used for
voltage design and local forecasting. Also included is an
economic appraisal, a study of the distribution system and an
assessment of the provision to low-income housing. Conclusions
and recommendations on future strategies complete the report.

ELECTRICAL DISTRIBUTION/ECONOMICS/MEXICO

8402

INVESTIGATION INTO THE PROVISION OF LOW COST
ELECTRICITY SUPPLY TO SERVE SITE AND SERVICES
HOUSING PROJECTS AT ASSIUT AND ALEXANDRIA

GILMORE HANKEY KIRKE CONSULTANTS 1978   pp35
(KIRKE J. AND WILLIAMS A.)

Power

Unpublished report for
URBAN PROJECTS DIVISION
WORLD BANK
WASHINGTON DC

The report details the needs analysis carried out to establish the
need for a supply (likely demand) and whether it could be afforded
by the community. The design approach for medium and low
voltage systems is described together with the layout of the
distribution system, transformer design and street lighting. An
estimate of costs is also presented.

AFFORDABILITY/TRANSFORMERS/EGYPT/
STREET LIGHTING

SEE 1406
SEE 1410
SEE 1413
SEE 1412
SEE 1420
SEE 1424

Section 9.

KEYWORDS

AAAAAAA

ABSORPTION DRAINS
6126

ABSTRACTION (OPTIONS)
5101

ACCESS
1102 1103 1104 1108 1110 1111 1203 1204 1404 1407
1416
4102 4105 4106 4120 4202 4401
6304

AFFORDABILITY
1110 1201 1203 1205 1206 1208 1217 1219 1222 1232
1405 1420
7406
8402

AFRICA
7307

AQUA PRIVY
1204 1407
6101 6103 6106 6107 6109 6117 6121 6125 6130 6131
6205 6209 6214 6215 6408 6413 6414 6417 6418 6419
6406 6422 6423 6425

AUTO FLUSH
6301

ASPHALT
3102

BBBBBBBBB

BANGLADESH
1408
6112

BENEFITS
1212 5209

BITUMEN ROADS
4113 4114 4116 4118 4119

BLOCK PAVING
4108 4110 4117

BOREHOLE LATRINES
6103

BOLIVIA
6120

BOTSWANA
1234
6111 6115 6133 6203 6304 6306 6422 6438

BRAZIL
1236 1419
5203 5206
6111 6120 6132

BUCKET LATRINE
6101 6103 6106 6130 6131 6205 6209 6216 6313 6403
6408 6413 6414 6416 6418 6423 6424 6425

BUILDINGS
3105

BUILDING REGULATIONS
1106

CCCCCCCCCC

CABLES
8101 8106 8117

CANALS
1414

CESSPITS
6414

CHANNELS
3103 3104 3106 3110 3111 3113 3114 3115 3302 3403
6101

CHANNEL LINING
3103 3110 3114 3403

CIRCULATION
1108
4106 4120

CISTERNS
5305

COLLECTION
6138

COLUMBIA
1215
6120 6434
7408

COMMUNAL LATRINES
1414 1421 1424
5103
6101 6107 6117 6119 6125 6207 6401 6403 6404 6410
6416 6425 6426 6436

COMMUNITY PARTICIPATION
1103 1110 1205 1210 1211 1212 1215 1216 1217 1218
1221 1222 1224 1225 1226 1229 1231 1234 1235 1236123712381301
1304 1410 1430
3118 3204
5116 5112 5203 5205 5208 5210 5402 5404
6206 6308 6313
7201

COMPOSTING
7105 7301

COMPOST LATRINES
6103 6205 6422

COMPUTER SOFTWARE
5120

CONCRETE PAVING
4101 4103 4104 4107 4111 4113 4114 4116 4118 4308

CONSTRUCTION
2105
6303

CONSTRUCTION MANAGEMENT
6302

COSTA RICA
1430

COSTS
1111 1113 1201 1204 1206 1209 1212 1217 1221 1226
1238 1302 1403 1409 1412 1413 1415 1416 1418 1419
1420 1422 1425 1431
2201
3302
4108
5107 5116 5118 5201 5204 5205 5206 5207 5208 5209
5210 5402 5405 5407 5408
6102 6104 6106 6107 6111 6113 6118 6120 6129 6201
6202 6205 6208 6302 6304 6310 6312 6401 6412 6413
6414 6415 6416 6417 6419 6420 6429 6432 6433 6435
6437 6438
7104 7201 7302 7304 7308 7309 7311 7401 7406
8102 8116 8117 8118 8201

COST RECOVERY
1210 1211 1220 1230 1232 1402 1406 1426 6309

DERELICT LAND
2104

DESLUDGING
6404

DEVELOPMENT
1234

DISPOSAL
6138

DISTRIBUTION
5209

DRAINAGE
1102 1103 1107 1110 1111 1114 1207 1230 1414 1417
1421 1422 1424 1426 1431
3102 3103 3104 3105 3106 3108 3110 3111 3112 3113
3114 3115 3116 3202 3203 3204 3301 3302 3303 3401
3402 3403 3404
4113 4114 4116 4120 4301 4302 4305 4401
5113 5407
6418

DRAINFIELDS
6107

EARTH ROADS
4302

ECONOMICS
1429
5403
6202 6206
7105 7106
8107 8112 8201 8401

EFFLUENT
3402
6114 6122

EGYPT
1201 1208 1420
6311
7408
8402

ELECTRICAL STANDARDS
8108

ELECTRICAL DEMAND
8201

ELECTRICAL DISTRIBUTION
8101 8102 8103 8106 8107 8112 8113 8115 8117 8302
8401

ELECTRICITY SUPPLY
1101 1108 1111 1112 1204 1207 1413 1417

EL SALVADOR
1220 1234 1402

ENERGY
1104

ENVIRONMENTAL BUFFER ZONES
6204

ETHIOPIA
6433

EVAPOTRANSPIRATION BEDS
6109 6122 6125

FFFFFFFFF

———

FERRO CEMENT
3302

FINANCE
1110 1113 1207 1210 1222 1225 1226 1230 1238 1303
1401 1413 1420
5103
6112 6210 6212 6308 6310 6403 6435
7101 7103 7403

FIRE HYDRANTS
1105
5108

FLOOD PREVENTION
1105

FOOTPATHS
1102 1105 1407

FOUNDATIONS
1107

GGGGGGGGGGGGG

———

GENERATION
7406 7407

GEOTEXTILES
3104

GHANA
1211 1305
6111 6301 6418

GRAVEL ROADS
4113 4116 4119 4303

GROUND FILL
1107
2105

GROUND PREPARATION
1103 1110 1207

GROUND WATER POLLUTION
6108

GUATEMALA
1430 1431
6434

HHHHHHHHH

———

HAITI
6434

HANDPUMPS
5101 5102 5119 5112 5306

HEALTH
3201 3303
5104 5201
6136

HONDURAS
1409

HONG KONG
1407

HOUSING DENSITY
1227 1237

HOUSE CONNECTIONS
5114

HOUSE SEWERS
6134

HOUSEHOLDS
1206

HYDRAULIC FILL
2101 2104

HYDRAULICS
1107
5120

IIIIIIII
———

IMPLEMENTATION
1223 1306 1406 1411 1425 1428 1431
5405
6308 6309 6313

INDIA
1106 1202 1212 1220 1224 1301 1304 1403 1404 1405
1417 1421 1422 1423 1424
2102
6114 6116 6202 6207 6210 6211 6212 6216 6308 6310
6313 6403 6424 6432 6435
7101 7104 7307 7308 7310 7408

INDIVIDUAL WATER CONNECTIONS
5117 5205 5408

INDONESIA
1221
5402 5408 5409
6120 6404 6423 6426
7307 7408

INFRASTRUCTURE
1201 1202 1208 1210 1211 1212 1213 1214 1215 1216
1218 1221 1223 1224 1225 1226 1228 1230 1231 1232
1233 1236 1302 1303 1403 1406 1408 1409 1410 1413
1414 1415 1418 1420 1423 1429

INSTITUTIONS
1205 1206 1430
5203 5210
6206

INTERACTIONS
1103

INTERCEPTOR TANKS
6118 6127 6433

IRAN
3113
7307 7402

ISRAEL
7405

JJJJJJJJJ
———

JORDAN
5403
6201

KKKKKK
——

KENYA
1412
5109 5205
6312 6413 6414 6415 6405 6406

LLLLLLLLL
———

LANDFILL
6130
7303 7305 7310 7408

LAND PRICING
1203

LATRINES
6302 6402

LAYOUT
1237 1404
4105

LEACH FIELDS
6125

LEACH PITS
6404

LESOTHO
1406
6133

LIBERIA
1216

LIGHTING
8105 8114

LOW VOLUME FLUSH W.C.
6116

MMMMMMMM
——

MALAYSIA
5103
6437

MALDIVES
3404 5405

MAINTENANCE
1230 1301 1303 1305 1414 1415 1431
3118
4104 4107 4110 4113 4117 4302 4303 4304
5102 5110 5111 5118 5208 5209 5301 5302 5303 5304
5305 5306 5402 5406
6107 6113 6115 6118 6120 6121 6122 6126 6130 6137
6208 6209 6301 6303 6304 6310 6312 6403 6417 6419
6404 6425 6427 6429 6435
7201
8101 8118

MANAGEMENT
1209
6201 6213

MARKETING
6411

MEXICO
6434
8401

MOZAMBIQUE
6402

MULTI TAP
5117

NNNNNNNN
———

NETWORK ANALYSIS
5110

NICARAGUA
1234 1427
6434

NIGERIA
3303 3403
6118 6408 6409 6412 6416 6417 6427 6428
7401

OOOOOOOOO
———

ON SITE SANITATION
6108 6136

OPEN SPACE
1105

OPERATION
1209 1230 1303 1401 1414 1415 1431
5108 5111 5208 5209 5301 5305 5306 5402

6115 6117 6122 6130 6137 6139 6201 6203 6208 6209
6303 6304 6310 6312 6403 6404 6417 6419 6427 6435
7308
OPTIONS
5206
6313

OVERHEAD LINES
8103 8104 8301

OVER HUNG LATRINES
6103

PPPPPPPPP
———

PAKISTAN
1223 1225 1426
6120 6132 6401 6429 6430 6431
7406 7407

PAPUA NEW GUINEA
6407

PARKING
1102 1105
4106

PAVING
4118 4301

PAVEMENT DESIGN
4116

PEDESTRIANS
4401

PERCOLATION
3117
6102

PERU
1221

PHILIPPINES
1305 1306 1414 1418
5207
7404 7408

PHOTOVOLTAIC ELECTRICITY
8105 8114 8120

PIER LATRINE
6408

PIPES
1414
3404
5108 5109 5115 5117 5114 5205

6101

PIT EMPTYING
6304 6305 6312 6306 6307

PIT LATRINES
6101 6103 6104 6107 6130 6131 6205 6209 6214 6305
6307 6408 6413 6414 6416 6419 6422 6425 6434

PLANNING
1104

PLOT SIZE
1404
6437

POLLUTION
6103 6308

POUR FLUSH LATRINES
5103
6103 6104 6107 6112 6114 6202 6210 6211 6212 6214
6216 6310 6313 6401 6406 6410 6424 6430 6431 6432
6434 6435 6436

POWER LINES
1105

POWER LOADS
8112

POWER POLES
8104 8301

PRICE ELASTICITY
5202

PROGRAMME DEVELOPMENT
1304

POWER SUPPLY
1103 1107 1110 1233

PUBLIC TAPS
5408
6426

PUBLIC UTILITIES
4105

PUMPING
5110

PURIFICATION
5105

RRRRRRRRRRRR

———

RAINFALL
3107

REC II
6438

RECYCLING
7102 7103 7403 7408

REFUSE COLLECTION VEHICLES
7311

REUSE
3109

ROOF CATCHMENTS
5204

ROAD CONSTRUCTION
1111
4101 4104 4107 4108 4109 4110 4111 4112 4113 4114
4116 4117 4301 4302 4303 4306 4308

ROAD DESIGN
1102 1103 1105 1106 1107 1108 1110 1112 1113 1114
1204 1207 1233 1236 1414 1417 1421 1422 1424 1427
1431
3401 3404
4113 4114 4107 4119 4118 4120 4201 4202 4307
6208

ROAD MAINTENANCE
4304 4305

RUN OFF
3107

SSSSSSSSS

———

SANITATION
1103 1104 1106 1110 1111 1112 1113 1207 1228 1230
1233 1414 1417
5104 5203 5206 5304 5405
6128 6308

SANITATION OPTIONS
1114
5107 5407
6123 6206 6208 6215 6309 6311 6409 6412 6415 6405
6428

SANITATION UPGRADING
6107

SAN SALVADOR
6434

SEEPAGE BEDS

Keywords

STABILISED EARTH
4109 4113 4114 4116 4119

STABILISATION PONDS
5107
6101 6131 6137 6139

STANDARDS
1204 4101

STANDPOSTS
1414 1424
5103 5115 5117 5113 5114 5205 5208 5305 5401 5405
5406
6208

STONE PAVING
4101 4116 4119

STORAGE
5305

STORM DRAINAGE
1112 1204 1236
6427 6431

STORM SEWERS
3116

STORMWATER OPTIONS
1104 1108 1408
3103 3110 3112 3113
5107
6135 6208 6215

STREET CLEANSING
7101 7305 7306

STREET LIGHTING
1102 1105 1111 1112 1204 1407 1424
8109 8110 8113 8116 8118 8119 8402

STRUCTURES
1107

SUB-STATIONS
8117 8301

SUDAN
5401 5406
6411

SULLAGE
1112 1207 1424 1427
3101 3117 3303 3402
5103 5107 5116 5407
6124 6128 6205 6208 6426 6431

SULLAGE DISPOSAL

3101 3109 3117 3201

SULLAGE TREATMENT
3117

SURFACE DRAINS
1407
6105 6208 6426

SURFACE WATER
6303

TTTTTTTTT
———

TANZANIA
1220 1425
4401
6111 6421
7409

TAPS
5113 5205
6208

TARIFFS
5202
7311

THAILAND
7309

TRANSFER STATIONS
7306

TRANSFORMERS
8101 8106 8402

TRANSPORTATION
1104

TUNISIA
6420

UUUUUUUUU
———

UGANDA
5407
8115

UNDERGROUND CABLES
8111 8115

UNITED ARAB EMIGRATES
3401

UK

1101 1102 1109
2106 2201

URBAN AREAS
3118

USA
1105
6124 6128 6213

UPGRADING
1103 1110 1205 1206 1211 1212 1221 1222 1224 1225
1226 1233 1238 1407 1410 1424 1427

UPPER VOLTA
1428

VVVVVVVV
——

VACUUM TRUCKS
6304 6306 6307 6312 6423

VALVES
5113 5115 5205

VAULTS
6101 6103 6106 6112 6209 6401 6413 6426 6436

VEHICLES
4202
7301 7305 7306

VENDORS
5401 5406

VIDP
6115 6203

VIP
6103 6107 6111 6113 6406 6411 6421

WWWWWWWWWWW
———

WASHING SLABS
3101 5407

WASTEWATER
6118 6131 6138 6213 6433

WATER DISTRIBUTION
5106 5105 5109 5110 5114 5115 5120 5207 5209 5210

WATER SEAL LATRINES
6313

WATER STORAGE
1105

5105 5109 5114 5204 5402 5409

WATER MAINS
5106 5403

WATER SUPPLY
1101 1103 1104 1105 1106 1107 1108 1110 1111 1112
1113 1114 1204 1207 1228 1230 1233 1236 1407 1409
1414 1417 1422 1426 1427 1431
5104 5107 5111 5116 5119 5203 5205 5206 5208 5209
5302 5303 5301 5304 5305 5306 5401 5402 5404 5405
5406 5407 5408 5409
6202 6208 6215 6418 6404

WATER TANKS
1414
5115 5118 5305 5405

WATER USE
5202

WC
6133 6207 6425

WATER WASTE DISPOSAL
1409
5111

WELLS
1414
5102 5108 5119 5305 5405

WIRING
8108

YYYYYYYY
——

YARD TAPS
5114

YEMEN
1415

ZZZZZZZZZ
——

ZAMBIA
1221 1401
6118 6120 6131 6419 6425 6436

ZIMBABWE
6111 6113

AUTHORS

KARPE H.J.	6101	MONAHAN E. J.	2105
KASS J.C.	6208	MORGAN P.R.	6113
KAUFMAN J.E.	8110	MORROW D.	6423
KELLARMAN A.	7405	MUKHERJEE S.K.	1403
KELLET P.	1215	MULLIGANIH van	5402
KEZDI A.	4109	MURTHY C.K.	8302
KHANNA P N	1107	MURTHY C.R.N.	8302
KHARE S.T.	6310	MURTHY K.R.	8302
KHELIL, AMAR	3202	MYERS M.	1220 1221
KING S.Y.	8111	NADGIR K.N.	8302
KINNEAR J.	5202	NATH K.J.	6424 7104 7308
KINORI B.Z.	3110		7310
KNAPTON J.	4110	NATIONAL BUILDING RESEARCH	
KONCKE C.	1215	INSTITUTE, REPUBLIC OF SOUTH	
KOPPELMAN L.	1105	AFRICA	1108
KSHIRSAGAR S.R.	6308	NEBIKER J.H.	3113
KUBOTA H.	7105	NEWMAN J.O.	6127
		NICHOLS P.	5406
		NIELSEN J.H.	6208
LACEY L.	1216	NIHON SUIDO CONSULTANTS	6426
LAKERVI E.	8112	NIMPUNO K.	3203
LALANDE F.	6420	NIYOGI S.	6114
LANGENEGGER O.	5101	NJAU F.Z.	6309
LANOIX J.N.	5119 6214	NOAH J.I.	6427
LAPIDOT M.	7405	NOSTRAND van J.	6115
LAQUIAN A.A.	1217		
LAURIA D.T.	5117 5206		
LELIAVSKY S.	3111	ODIER L	4113
LEMAN GROUP INC	4401	OECD	4201
LEVE G.	1218	OGLESBY C.H.	4114
LEWIS W.J	6108	OKUBADEJO A.O.	3303
LILLEY A.A.	4111	OKUN D.A.	5209
LINDEN van der J.	1219 1223 1225	OLSSON E.	6116
LLOYD B	6119	OLUWANDE P.A.	3303 6117 6428
LOHANI B.N.	7103	ONIBOKUN A.	6428
		ORANGI PILOT PROJECT	6429 6430
		OTIS R.J.	6118
MABUBA P.B.	5118	OUANO E.A.R	7309
MAJUMBER N.	6207	OVERSEAS DEVELOPMENT	
MAKERERE D.J.	6421	ADMINISTRATION	1420 1421 1422
MANN H.T.	6109	OWUSU S.E.	1216
MANOHARN S.	3302	OXFAM/MARSTON	6119
MARA D.D.	3201 6107 6110	O'REILLY M.P.	4116
	6111 6113 6118		
	6205 6416 6417		
	6418 6419	PACEY A.	6209
MARIAS van G. R.	6131	PARKMAN CONSULTING ENGINEERS	5407
MARSDEN D.	1304	PARLATO R.	6210
MATHEY K.	1419	PARRY J.	1110
McCOMBE J.	8301	PATHAK B.	6211
McGARRY M.	6123	PAYNE G.	1207
McNELIS B.	8114	PAYNE G.K.	1222
MEHRA S.R.	4113	PELTENBURG M.	1223
MENEZES L.	1220 1221	PICKFORD J.A.	5303 6121 6431
MENON S.G.	8113		6120
MILLARD R.	7306	POLPRASERT C.	6122 6123
MILLARD R.S.	4112 4116 4113	PONNIAH C.D.	5103
MOES W.	6112	POSTMA S.F.	5408
MOLEN van der W.H.	3108	PURDY M.T.	2106

Authors

RABBANI K.R.	7105			
RAJ DEV	6432			
RAJPUT, V.S.	6122			
RAMAMURTHY K.N.	1224			
RAO B.	8113			
RAU B.B.	6310	6432		
REED R.A.	6431	6120		
	6132			
ROBERTS M.	1111			
ROCHE R.	5101			
ROMANN D.	1112			
RONEN R.	7405			
ROY A.K.	6212	6310	6432	
ROY K.	1423			
ROY S.K.	1423			
RYBCZYNSKI W.	1404	4202	6123	
RYN van der S.	6124			
SAE-HAU U.	1402			
SAHLE H.	6433			
SALINAS B.	6434			
SALLY H.L.	3114			
SANTOS P.D.	4113			
SANYAUB	1401			
SARMA Bh.V.	1424			
SATTERTHWAITE DAVID	1214			
SAULEZ K.J.	8115			
SCHALEKAMP M.	5409			
SCHILDERMAN T.	3301			
SCHILLER E.J.	5301	6125		
SCHOORL J.W.	1225			
SCHROEDER D.M.	6403			
SECKINGTON C.C.	3404			
SHAHALAM M.	6201			
SHANKLAND COX PARTNERSHIP	1226			
SHETTY M.S.	6126	8302		
SHIPMANN H.	5304			
SIEBOLDS P.	1425			
SIKANDER S.	1426			
SILVA R.T.	1427			
SIMMONS J.D.	6127			
SIMPSON B.J.	2106			
SINGH R.S.	6310			
SINNATAMBY G.N.	7406			
SINNATAMBY G.S.	6110			
SIVARAMAKRISHNAN K.C.	1220	1221		
SKINNER R.J.	1301			
SOIL CONSERVATION SERVICE	3115			
SRIDHAR M.K.C.	3303			
SRI LANKA MINISTRY OF HIGHWAYS	4303			
STARR M.	8114			
STEINBERG F.	1425			
STEVENS P.H.M.	1227			
STEVENS W.R.	8116			
STOCK A.F.	4117			
STONER C.H.	6128			

SUESS M.J.	7106			
SULABH S.	6435			
SUNDARESAN B.B.	7301			
SWAFFIELD J.A.	6133			
TAYLOR E.O.	8117			
TARIQ K.	7406			
THAKUR B.B.	7310			
THERKELSEN H.	6106			
THOMAS P.R.	1224			
TODD D.M.	6436			
TRANS AND ROAD RES LABORATORY	3116	4118	4119	
	4304	4305	4306	
	4307	4308		
TSCHANNEREL G.	5101			
UNCHS	1113	1114	1228	
	1229	1230	1231	
	1232	1233	3204	
	4120	6129	7311	
UNDESA	1428			
UNITED KINGDOM NATIONAL JOINT UTILITIES GROUP	1109			
URBAN EDGE	1234	1305	6216	
	6312	7201	7408	
UNITED STATES AGENCY FOR INTERNATIONAL DEVELOPMENT	5305	6130		
UUJAMHAN	6134			
VALVERDE N.	1401			
VINCENT L.J.	6131			
VINES M.	6120	6132		
VIRARAGHAVAN, T	6122	6213		
WAGNER E.C.	5119	6214		
WAKELIN R.H.M.	6133	6134		
WALDRAM J.M.	8118			
WANG. B.C.C.	6437			
WARD P.	1235			
WARNER D.B.	6311			
WATER AND SANITATION FOR HEALTH	5306	6215		
WATER POLLUTION CONTROL FEDERATION	6135			
WEBBER D.	6119			
WEHENPOHL G.	1236			
WHEELER D.	6136			
WICKRAMASENA A.K.A.	1429			
WILLIAMS D.F.	6403			
WILLIAMSON G	1237			
WILSON J.G.	6115	6438		
WINNEBERGER J.H.T.	3117			
WORLD BANK PUBLIC UTILITIES NOTE	5210			
WORLD BANK INTERREG PROJECT	5120			
WORLD BANK PAPER	1238			
WORLD HEALTH ORGANISATION	3118	6313	6138	
	6137			

ADDRESSES

A
-

AMERICAN PLANNING ASSOCIATION.
1776 MASSACHUSETTS AVENUE
N.W. WASHINGTON D.C. 20036
U.S.A.

AMERICAN SOCIETY OF CIVIL ENGINEERS (A.S.C.E.).
345 EAST 47th STREET
NEW YORK 10017-2398
U.S.A.

ANGLO AMERICAN COUNCIL ON PRODUCTIVITY.
21 TOTHILL STREET
LONDON SW1
ENGLAND.

ANN ARBOR SCIENCE PUBLISHERS.
230 COLLINGWOOD
P.O.BOX 1425
ANN ARBOR
MICHIGAN 48106
U.S.A.

ARCHITECTURAL PRESS.
9 QUEEN ANNE'S GATE
LONDON SW1H 9BY
ENGLAND

ARDHI INSTITUTE.
CENTRE FOR HOUSING STUDIES
P.O. BOX 35124
DAR ES SALAAM
UNITED REPUBLIC OF TANZANIA.

ATHENS CENTRE OF EKISTICS.
ATHENS TECHNOLOGICAL ORGANISATION
24 STRAT SYNDESMOU
ATHENS 136
GREECE

ASIAN INSTITUTE OF TECHNOLOGY (A.I.T.).
P.O. BOX 2754
BANGKOK 10501
THAILAND.

B
-

BAPTIE SHAW AND MORTON.
95 BOTHWELL STREET
GLASGOW G2 7HX
SCOTLAND.

BINNIE AND PARTNERS.
GROSVENOR HOUSE
69 LONDON ROAD
REDHILL
SURREY RH1 1LQ
ENGLAND.

BKH CONSULTING ENGINEERS.
ABRAHAM PATRASSTRAAT 5
P.O. BOX 93224
2509 AE THE HAGUE
THE NETHERLANDS.

BRITISH CEMENT ASSOCIATION (B.C.A.).
WEXHAM SPRINGS
SLOUGH SL3 6PL
ENGLAND.

BRITISH STANDARDS INSTITUTION (B.S.I.).
LINFORD WOOD
MILTON KEYNES MK14 6LE
ENGLAND.

BUILDING RESEARCH ESTABLISHNENT (B.R.E.).
BUCKNALLS LANE
GARSTON
WATFORD WD2 7JR
ENGLAND.

BUTTERWORTHS & Co. (PUBLISHERS)Ltd.
BOROUGH GREEN
SEVENOAKS
KENT TN15 8PH
ENGLAND.

C
-

CAPRA PRESS.
631 STATE STREET
SANTA BARBARA
CALIFORNIA 93101
U.S.A.

CEMENT AND CONCRETE ASSOCIATION.
(SEE BRITISH CEMENT ASSOCIATION)

(C.E.P.I.S.)
see PAN AMERICAN CENTRE FOR
SANITARY ENGINEERING.

CENTRAL PUBLIC HEALTH ENGINEERING RESEARCH
INSTITUTE (C.P.H.E.R.I.)
NEHRU MARG
NAGPUR 3
INDIA.

CHAPMAN & HALL.
ASSOCIATED BOOK PUBLISHERS Ltd.
11 FETTER LANE
LONDON EC4P 4EE
ENGLAND.

COMMONWEALTH SCIENTIFIC AND INDUSTRIAL
RESEARCH ORGANISATION (C.S.I.R.O.)
PORT MORESBY OFFICE
BOROKO
PAPUA NEW GUINEA.

CONSTRUCTION PRESS. see LONGMANS (PUBLISHERS)

COWI CONSULT.
45 TEKNIKERBYEN 2830
VIRUM
DENMARK.

D
-

(D.O.T.) DEPARTMENT OF TRANSPORT. U.K.

(D.O.E.) DEPARTMENT OF THE ENVIRONMENT. U.K.

DEVELOPMENT PLANNING UNIT (D.P.U.)
UNIVERSITY COLLEGE LONDON
9 ENDSLEIGH GARDENS
LONDON WCIH OED
ENGLAND.

E
-

EDWARD ARNOLD (publishers)
41 BEDFORD SQUARE
LONDON WC1B 3DQ
ENGLAND.

ELSEVIER APPLIED SCIENCE (PUBLISHERS).
CROWN HOUSE
LINTON ROAD
BARKING
ESSEX 1G11 8JU
ENGLAND.

ENGINEERING PUBLISHERS.
P.O.BOX 725
NEW DEHLI 110001
INDIA.

ENGINEERING SCIENCE.
125 WEST HUNTINGTON DRIVE
P.O. BOX 538
ARCADIA
CALIFORNIA 91006
U.S.A.

ENGLISH UNIVERSITY PRESS.
WARWICK LANE
LONDON EC4
ENGLAND.

ENVIRONMENTAL SANITATION INFORMATION
CENTRE (E.N.S.I.C.)
ASIAN INSTITUTE OF TECHNOLOGY
P.O. BOX 2754
BANGKOK 10501
THAILAND.

F
-

FOOD AND AGRICULTURE ORGANISATION OF THE
UNITED NATIONS (F.A.O.).
VIA DELLE TERME DI CRARCALLA
00100 ROME
ITALY.

FRENCH AGENCY FOR OVERSEAS MANAGEMENT
AND DEVELOPMENT.
ACA 98
rue de l'universite - 75007
PARIS
FRANCE.

FUEL AND METALLURGICAL JOURNALS.
QUEENSWAY HOUSE
2 QUEENSWAY
REDHILL
SURREY RH1 1QS
ENGLAND

G
-

GILMORE HANKEY KIRKE.
ST. JAMES HALL
MOOR PARK ROAD
LONDON SW6
ENGLAND.

H
-

HUMAN SETTLEMENTS MANAGEMENT INSTITUTE.
212 ASIAN GAMES VILLAGE COMPLEX
KHELGA MARG
NEW DEHLI - 110049
INDIA.

HOUSING AND URBAN DEVELOPMENT CORPORATION
(H.U.D.C.O.)
HUDCO HOUSE
LODHI ROAD
NEW DEHLI 110003

INDIA.
HER MAJESTYS STATIOERY OFFICE (HMSO)
P.O. BOX 276
LONDON SW8 5DT
ENGLAND.

I
-

ILIFFE BOOKS.
DORSET HOUSE
STAMFORD STREET
LONDON SE1
ENGLAND.

ILLUMINATING SOCIETY OFF NORTH AMERICA.
345 EAST 47th STREET
NEW YORK 10017
U.S.A.

INDIAN SCIENTIFIC DOCUMENTATION CENTRE
(INDSOC).
14 SATSANG VIHAR MARG
OFF S.J.S. SAN SANWAL MARG
NEW DEHLI 110067
INDIA.

THE INSTITUTE OF ENGINEERS (INDIA)
8 GOKHALE ROAD
CALCUTTA 700200
INDIA.

THE INSTITUTE OF MILITARY ENGINEERS (INDIA)
PONNA
INDIA.

THE INSTITUTION OF CIVIL ENGINEERS (I.C.E.)
1-7 GREAT GEORGE STREET
LONDON SW1P 3AA
ENGLAND.

THE INSTITUTION OF ELECTRICAL ENGINEERS
PUBLICATIONS DEPARTMENT
P.O. BOX 8
SOUTHGATE HOUSE
STEVENAGE
HERTS SG1 1HQ
ENGLAND

INSTITUTION OF LIGHTING ENGINEERS
LENNOX HOUSE
9 LAWFORD ROAD, RUGBY
CV21 2DZ
ENGLAND

THE INSTITUTION OF MUNICIPAL ENGINEERS
(SEE THE INSTITUTUION OF CIVIL ENGINEERS.)

THE INSTITUTION OF WATER ENGINEERS AND
SCIENTISTS (I.W.E.S.)
31-33 HIGH HOLBORN
LONDON WC1V 6AX
ENGLAND.

INTERMEDIATE TECHNOLOGY PUBLICATIONS.
103-105 SOUTHAMPTON ROW
LONDON WC1B 4HH
ENGLAND.

INTERNATIONAL DEVELOPMENT RESEARCH CENTRE
(I.D.R.C.)
60 QUEENS STREET
P.O. BOX 8500
OTTAWA
ONTARIO K1G 3H9
CANADA.

INTERNATIONAL INSTITUTE FOR LANDS,
RECLAMATION AND IMPROVEMENT
P.O. BOX 45
6700 AA WAGENINGEN
THE NETHERLANDS

INTERNATIONAL REFERENCE CENTRE FOR
WASTES DISPOSAL (I.R.C.W.D.)
UEBERLANDSTRASSE 133
CH 8600 DUEBENDORF
SWITZERLAND.

INTERNATIONAL REFERNCE CENTRE FOR
COMMUNITY WATER SUPPLY AND SANITATION (IRC).
PRINSES MARGRIETPLANTSOEN 20
P.O. BOX 93190
2509 AD THE HAGUE
THE NETHERLANDS.

INTERNATIONAL UNION OF PRODUCERS AND
DISTRIBUTORS OF ELECTRICAL ENERGY
(I.U.P.D.E.E.)
3 AVENUE DE FRIEDLAND
PARIS 8
FRANCE.

(I.B.R.D.) see WORLD BANK.

(I.Y.S.H.) INTERNATIONAL YEAR OF SHELTER
FOR THE HOMELESS.

J
-

JOHNS HOPKINS PUBLISHERS.
EUROPEAN BOOK SERVICE Ltd.
ST. LEONARDS HOUSE
WEST MALLING
KENT ME19 6PE

Addresses

ENGLAND.
L
-

LIVERPOOL UNIVERSITY PRESS
P.O. BOX 147
LIVERPOOL L69 3BX
ENGLAND

LONGMANS
LONGMANS HOUSE
BURNT MILL
HARLOW
ESSEX CM20 2JE
ENGLAND.

M
-

MACDONALD & Co. (PUBLISHERS)
3rd FLOOR
GREATER LONDON HOUSE
HAMPSTEAD ROAD
LONDON NW1 7QX
ENGLAND.

McGILL UNIVERSITY.
MacDONALD COLLEGE
DEPARTMENT OF RENEWABLE RESOURCES
21.111 LAKESIDE ROAD
STE ANNE DE BELLEVUE
QUEBEC
CANADA.

McGILL UNIVERSITY.
CENTRE FOR MINIMUM COST HOUSING
3550 UNIVERSITY STREET
MONTREAL
QUEBEC H3A 2A7
CANADA.

MINISTRY OF LOCAL GOVERNMENT AND LANDS.
DEVELOPMENT HOUSE
GABORONE
BOTSWANA.

N
-

NATIONAL BUILDING RESEARCH INSTITUTE
(N.B.R.I.)
P.O. BOX 395
PRETORIA
SOUTH AFRICA.

NATIONAL ENVIRONMENTAL ENGINEERING
RESEARCH INSTITUTE (NEERI).
NEHRU MARG
NAGPUR 440 020
INDIA.

NATIONAL HOUSING AUTHORITY.
CHILUFYA MULENGA ROAD
P.O. BOX 50074
LUSAKA
ZAMBIA.

THE NATIONAL SWEDISH INSTITUTE FOR
BUILDING RESEARCH.
BOX 785
S-801 29 GALVE
SWEDEN.

NATIONAL WATER SUPPLY AND DRAINAGE BOARD,
SRI LANKA

NIHON SUIDO CONSULTANTS

O
-

ORANGI PILOT PROJECT.
DAULAT HOUSE
ORANGI TOWN
KARACHI
PAKISTAN.

OVERSEAS DEVELOPMENT ADMINISTRATION. (ODA)
ELAND HOUSE
STAG PLACE
LONDON
ENGLAND.

OXFAM.
274 BANBURY ROAD
OXFORD
ENGLAND.

P
-

PAN AMERICAN CENTRE FOR SANITARY
ENGINEERING AND ENVIRONMENTAL SCIENCES
(CEPIS).
P.O. BOX 4337
LIMA 100
PERU.

PARKMAN CONSULTING ENGINEERS.
CUNARD BUILDING
LIVERPOOL L3 1ES
ENGLAND.

PAVLAVI UNIVERSITY
SCHOOL OF ENGINEERING
DEPARTMENT OF CIVIL ENGINEERING
SHIRAZ
IRAN.

PERGAMMON PRESS
HEADINGTON HILL HALL
OXFORD OX3 OBW
ENGLAND.

PLANNING TRANSPORT RESEARCH AND
COMPUTATION (P.T.R.C.)
PTRC EDUCATION RESEARCH SERVICES Ltd.
110 STRAND
LONDON WC2
ENGLAND.

* POLYTEKNIK FORLAG

R
-

RODALE PRESS
E MINOR STREET
P.A. 18049
U.S.A.

THE ROSS INSTITUTE OF TROPICAL HYGIENE.
LONDON SCHOOL OF HYGIENE AND
TROPICAL MEDICINE
KEPPEL/GOWER STREET
LONDON WC1E 7HT
ENGLAND.

S
-

SATYA PRAKASHAN
16/7698 NEW MARKET
NEW ROHTAK ROAD
NEW DEHLI 110005
INDIA.

SHANKLAND COX.
16 BEDFORD SQUARE
LONDON WCIB 3JH
ENGLAND.

STERLING PUBLICATIONS
2 PARK AVENUE
NEW YORK 10016
U.S.A.

SULABH INTERNATIONAL.
PATNA SOUTH GANDHI
MAIDAN PATNA 800001
BIHAR
INDIA.

(S.D.D.) SCOTTISH DEVELOPMENT DEPARTMENT.

T
-

TAMPERE UNIVERSITY OF TECHNOLOGY.
P.O. BOX 527
33101 TAMPERE
FINLAND.

THOMAS TELFORD.
THOMAS TELFORD HOUSE
1 HERON QUAY
LONDON E14 9XF
ENGLAND.

TRANSPORT AND ROAD RESEARCH
LABORATORY (T.R.R.L.).
OLD WOKINGHAM ROAD
CROWTHORNE
BERKSHIRE RG11 6AU
ENGLAND.

TRIALOG.
PLOENNIESSTR. 18
D - 6100 DARMSTADT
FEDERAL REPUBLIC OF GERMANY.

U
-

UNITED NATIONS CENTRE FOR
HUMAN SETTLEMENTS (U.N.C.H.S.)
P.O. BOX 30030
NAIROBI
KENYA.

UNITED NATIONS CHILDRENS FUND (U.N.I.C.E.F.)
866 UNITED NATIONS PLAZA
NEW YORK NY 10017
UNITED STATES.

UNITED STATES AGENCY FOR
INTERNATIONAL DEVELOPMENT (U.S.A.I.D.)
WASHINGTON DC 20523
UNITED STATES.

UNITED STATES DEPARTMENT OF AGRICULTURE.
GIFFORD PINCHOT DRIVE
P.O. BOX 5130
MADISON WI 53705
UNITED STATES.

UNIVERSITY OF BIRMINGHAM.
DEVELOPMENT ADMINISTRATION GROUP
P.O. BOX 363
BIRMINGHAM B15 2TT
ENGLAND.

UNIVERSITY OF CHICAGO PRESS
11030 S LANGLEY AVENUE
CHICAGO
ILLINOIS 60628
U.S.A.

UNIVERSITY OF DORTMUND.
INSTITUTE OF ENVIRONMENTAL PROTECTION
P.O. BOX 500500
4600 DORTMUND 50
FEDERAL REPUBLIC OF GERMANY.

UNIVERSITY OF LEEDS
DEPARTMENT OF CIVIL ENGINEERING
LEEDS LS2 9JT
ENGLAND.

UNIVERSITY OF NAIROBI.
HOUSING RESEARCH AND DEVELOPMENT UNIT
P.O. BOX 30197
NAIROBI
KENYA.

UNIVERSITY OF NAIROBI.
DEPARTMENT OF CIVIL ENGINEERING
P.O. BOX 30197
NAIROBI
KENYA.

UNIVERSITY OF NORTH CAROLINA
DEPARTMENT OF ENVIRONMENTAL
SCIENCES AND ENGINEERING
SCHOOL OF PUBLIC HEALTH
CHAPEL HILL
NORTH CAROLINA 27514
U.S.A.

V
-

VAN NOSTRAND REINHOLD PUBLISHERS
MOLLY MILLARS LANE
WOKINGHAM
BERKS RG11 2PY
ENGLAND.

W
-

WATER AND SANITATION FOR
HEALTH PROJECT (W.A.S.H.)
1611 NORTH KENT STREET
ARLINGTON
VA 22209
UNITED STATES.

WATER, ENGINEERING AND DEVELOPMENT
CENTRE (W.E.D.C.).
UNIVERSITY OF TECHNOLOGY
LOUGHBOROUGH
LEICESTERSHIRE
ENGLAND.

WATER RESEARCH CENTRE (W.R.C.).
P.O. BOX 16
HENLEY ROAD
MEDMENHAM
MARLOW
BUCKS SL7 2HD
ENGLAND.

JOHN WILEY & SONS Ltd.
BAFFINS LANE
CHICHESTER
WEST SUSSEX PO19 1UD
ENGLAND.

WORLD HEALTH ORGANISATION (W.H.O.)
de la SANTE
AVENUE APPIA
1211 GENEVA 27
SWITZERLAND.

WORLD HEALTH ORGANISATION (.W.H.O.).
EASTERN MEDITERRANEAN REGIONAL OFFICE
P.O. BOX 1517
ALEXANDRIA 21511
EYGPT.

WORLD HEALTH ORGANISATION (W.H.O.).
REGIONAL OFFICE FOR SOUTH EAST ASIA
WORLD HEALTH HOUSE
NEW DEHLI 110 002
INDIA.

WORLD BANK.
ECONOMIC DEVELOPMENT INSTITUTE (E.D.I.)
1800 G STREET N.W.
WASHINGTON DC 20433
UNITED STATES.

WORLD BANK.
(INTERNATIONAL BANK FOR
RECONSTRUCTION AND
DEVELOPMENT, I.B.R.D.)
1818 H STREET NW
WASHINGTON DC 20433
UNITED STATES.

Sources Consulted

ABSTRACTS

GEOGRAPHY
URBAN
INSTITUTION OF CIVIL ENGINEERS
INTERNATIONAL CIVIL ENGINEER
ELECTRICAL ENGINEERING
INDEX TO SCIENTIFIC AND TECHNICAL PROCEEDINGS
INDEX TO SCIENTIFIC BOOK CONTENTS
SCIENCE CITATION INDEX
WATER RESEARCH CENTRE

INTERNATIONAL AGENCIES

ASIAN DEVELOPMENT BANK
CARIBBEAN DEVELOPMENT BANK
U.N.C.H.S.
U.N.E.S.C.O
U.N.I.D.O.
U.N.C.R.D.
WORLD BANK

GOVERNMENT DEPARTMENTS

O.D.A.
HUMAN SETTLEMENTS, ZAMBIA
LUSAKA URBAN DISTRICT COUNCIL, ZAMBIA
LUANSHYA DISTRICT COUNCIL, ZAMBIA
MADRAS METRO DEVELOPMENT AUTHORITY, INDIA
NATIONAL HOUSING CORPORATION. KENYA
NATIONAL URBAN DEVELOPMENT CORP.,INDONESIA
CAPITAL DEVELOPMENT AUTHORITY, TANZANIA
OFFICE OF THE PRESIDENT, MALAWI
MINISTRY OF LOCAL GOV. AND LANDS,BOTSWANA
HOUSING AND SETTLEMENT
DIRECTORATE,BANGLADESH
TOWN AND COUNTRY PLANNING DEPT. GHANA
URBAN DEVELOPMENT CORPORATION. JAMAICA
NATIONAL HOUSING AUTHORITY, LIBERIA
MINISTRY OF HOUSING AND LOCAL GOVERNMENT,
MALAYSIA
BHAKTAPUR DEVELOPMENT PROJECT, NEPAL
FED. MINISTRY OF WORKS AND HOUSING. NIGERIA
DEPARTMENT OF HOUSING. PAPUA NEW GUINEA
MINISTRY OF CONST. AND NAT.HOUSING, ZIMBABWE
NATIONAL HOUSING AUTHORITY, THAILAND
TECHNICAL SERVICES CENTRE, GHANA

CONSULTANTS

FRANK GRAHAM
HALCROW
HAISTE
ROUGHTON
SCOTT WILSON
ALLOT AND LOMAX
COLIN BUCHANAN
HUSBAN AND Co.
HUZZAR BRAMMAH
J.BURROW
PARKMAN
POSFORD DUVIVIER
ROFE KENNARD AND LAPWORTH
T.P.O"SULLIVAN
TRAVERS MORGAN
W.S. ATKINS
W.P.L.U.
TATA

UNIVERSITIES

O.D.I.
I.D.S.
BIRMINGHAM
HERRIOT WATT
BRADFORD
DUNDEE
EAST ANGLIA
NEWCASTLE UPON TYNE
NOTTINGHAM
SHEFFIELD
INSTITUTE FOR URBAN STUDIES, KENYA
CENTRE FOR DEVELOPMENT STUDIES, INDIA
ARDHI INSTITUTE, TANZANIA
COLLEGE OF MILITARY ENGINEERING, INDIA
ASIAN INSTITUTE OF TECHNOLOGY, THAILAND

CONFERENCES etc.

WATER, ENGINEERING AND DEVELOPMENT CENTRE
P.T.R.C.
INTER. CONF.ON ELECTRICAL DISTRIBUTION
REGIONAL SEMINAR ON SOLID WASTE, THAILAND
SEMINAR ON THE IMPLEMENTATION OF LOW-
COST SANITATION PROGRAMMES, TANZANIA
URBAN SHELTER IN DEVELOPING COUNTRIES
ASIAN WATER CONFERENCE, MALAYSIA
AFRICAN WATER CONFERENCE, KENYA

JOURNALS

EKISTICS
GEOGRAPHY
GEOGRAPHY AND THE URBAN ENVIRONMENT
GEOGRAPHICAL REVIEW
GEOGRAPHICAL MAGAZINE
GEOGRAPHICAL JOURNAL
THIRD WORLD QUARTERLY REVIEW
URBAN STUDIES
TOWN PLANNING REVIEW
AREA
JOURNAL OF TROPICAL GEOGRAPHY
URBAN GEOGRAPHY
NEW AFRICAN RESEARCH BULLETIN
APPLIED GEOGRAPHY
BUILT ENVIRONMENT
ENVIRONMENT AND PLANNING
JOUR. OF THE AMERICAN PLANNING ASSOC.
JOUR. OF THE ROYAL TOWN PLANNING INST.
PLANNER
TOWN AND COUNTRY
PROGRESS IN PLANNING
CHARTERED CIVIL ENGINEER
CHARTERED MUNICIPAL ENGINEER
CONSULTING ENGINEER U.K.
CONSULTING ENGINEER U.S.A.
CONSULTING ENGINEER INTERNATIONAL
PUBLIC HEALTH ENGINEER

MUNICIPAL ENGINEER
JOUR. OF THE AMERICAN WATER WORKS ASSOC.
AFRICAN WATER AND SEWERAGE
AQUA
ASIAN WATER AND SEWERAGE
NEW CIVIL ENGINEER
ENFO
ENSIC REVIEW
IRCWD NEWS
OPEN HOUSE INTERNATIONAL
HABITAT NEWS
HABITAT INTERNATIONAL
THIRD WORLD PLANNING REVIEW
WASTES MANAGEMENT
WATER LINES
WORLD WATER
CITIES
CONSERVATION AND RECYCLING
ENVIRONMENT
ENVIRONMENTALIST
ENVIRONMENT INTERNATIONAL
I.D.S. BULLETIN
JOURNAL OF ENVIRONMENTAL MANAGEMENT
JOUR. OF THE INSTITUTE OF ENG. INDIA
O.D.I REVIEW
PUBLIC WORKS
URBAN DEVEL. AND URBAN RENEWAL
WASTE MANAGEMENT

www.ingramcontent.com/pod-product-compliance
Ingram Content Group UK Ltd.
Pitfield, Milton Keynes, MK11 3LW, UK
UKHW050009160726
7214IPUK00018B/347

9 781853 391880